HERMES BOOKS

John Herington, Founding Editor

Also available in this series:

HERODOTUS

JAMES ROMM

FOREWORD BY JOHN HERINGTON

YALE UNIVERSITY PRESS
NEW HAVEN AND LONDON

Designed by Sally Harris.
Set in Palatino type by à la page, New Haven, Connecticut.
Printed in the United States of America by BookCrafters,
Inc., Chelsea, Michigan.

Library of Congress Cataloging-in-Publication Data

Romm, James S.
    Herodotus / James Romm ; foreword by John Herington.
      p. cm. — (Hermes books)
    Includes bibliographical references and index.
    ISBN 0-300-07229-5 (cloth: alk. paper)
          0-300-07230-9 (pbk.: alk. paper)
      1. Herodotus. 2. Herodotus. History. 3. History,
Ancient—Historiography. 4. Historians—Greece—
Biography. I. Title.
    D56.52.H45R66   1998
    938'.0072'02—dc21   98-10983
                                                    CIP

A catalogue record for this book is available from the British
Library.

The paper in this book meets the guidelines for permanence
and durability of the Committee on Production Guidelines
for Book Longevity of the Council on Library Resources.

10 9 8 7 6 5 4 3 2 1

FOR TANYA

. . . a chance which does redeem all sorrows
that ever I have felt.

—*King Lear*

CONTENTS

FOREWORD

"It would be a pity," said Nietzsche, "if the classics should speak to us less clearly because a million words stood in the way." His forebodings seem now to have been realized. A glance at the increasing girth of successive volumes of the standard journal of classical bibliography, *L'Année Philologique*, since World War II is enough to demonstrate the proliferation of writing on the subject in our time. Unfortunately, the vast majority of the studies listed will prove on inspection to be largely concerned with points of detail and composed by and for academic specialists in the field. Few are addressed to the literate but nonspecialist adult or to that equally important person, the intelligent but uninstructed beginning student; and of those few, very few indeed are the work of scholars of the first rank, equipped for their task not merely with raw classical erudition but also with style, taste, and literary judgment.

It is a strange situation. On one side stand the classical masters of Greece and Rome, those models of concision, elegance, and understanding of the human condition, who composed least of all for narrow technologists, most of all for the Common Reader (and, indeed, the Common Hearer). On the other side stands a sort of industrial complex, processing those masters into an annually growing output of technical articles and monographs. What is lacking, it seems, in our society as well as in our scholarship, is the kind of book that was supplied for earlier generations by such men as Richard Jebb and

Gilbert Murray in the intervals of their more technical researches—the kind of book that directed the general reader not
to the pyramid of secondary literature piled over the burial
places of the classical writers but to the living faces of the writers themselves, as perceived by a scholar-humanist with a
deep knowledge of, and love for, his subject. Not only for the
sake of the potential student of classics, but also for the sake of
humanities as a whole, within and outside academe, it seems
that this gap in classical studies ought to be filled. The Hermes
series is a modest attempt to fill it.

We have sought men and women possessed of a rather
rare combination of qualities: a love for literature in other languages, extending into modern times; a vision that extends beyond academe to contemporary life itself; and above all an
ability to express themselves in clear, lively, and graceful English, without polysyllabic language or parochial jargon. For
the aim of the series requires that they should communicate to
nonspecialist readers, authoritatively and vividly, their personal sense of why a given classical author's writings have ex-
cited people for centuries and why they can continue to do so.
Some are classical scholars by profession, some are not; each
has lived long with the classics, and especially with the author
about whom he or she writes in this series.

The first, middle, and last goal of the Hermes series is to
guide the general reader to a dialogue with the classical masters rather than to acquaint him or her with the present state
of scholarly research. Thus our volumes contain few or no
footnotes; even within the texts, references to secondary literature are kept to a minimum. At the end of each volume,
however, is a short bibliography that includes recommended
English translations, and selected literary criticism, as well
as historical and (when appropriate) biographical studies.

Throughout, all quotations from the Greek or Latin texts are given in English translation.

In these ways we hope to let the classics speak again, with a minimum of modern verbiage (as Nietzsche wished), to the widest possible audience of interested people.

John Herington

PREFACE

SOME OF THE BEST-LOVED STORIES IN LITERATURE ARE THOSE OF the largest scope, depicting not just an episode of human life but, behind that, a great era of history. Think for a moment of ancient epics like Homer's *Iliad* and Virgil's *Aeneid*, but also of novels like Hugo's *Les Misérables* and Tolstoy's *War and Peace*, or of films like *Doctor Zhivago* and *Gone with the Wind*. In each case the tale of a single person or pair of lovers has been set against the backdrop of a war or social upheaval, showing how history swirls around the lives of individuals and gives meaning to their sufferings and triumphs.

Now imagine taking this large-scope approach to storytelling and expanding it one level further: instead of one or two lives surrounded by war, take the war itself as protagonist and show it surrounded by the entire world. The result, I think, would look very much like Herodotus's *Histories*. For the *Histories* is a story, but the story of an era, not of a person, and it is staged against the backdrop of the earth itself. Unlike other storytellers, Herodotus dares to expand his scope as far as it will go, reaching the limit of the known in both space and time, dwarfing the scale of the individual human life.

This is not to say that the *Histories* disregards individuals, for indeed, Herodotus is fascinated by them. But he views them from a great distance, telescoping their victories, loves, and losses—episodes that could each have easily filled out a modern-day novel—into only a paragraph or two of text. None survive through more than a third of the *Histories*, so that none can be called its hero, the person whom the story is "about." Instead, it is the war that endures: a conflict between East and West stretching back into prehistory and progressing with rising intensity through some eighty years of historical time. Three generations come and go during its lifespan, and even those present at its conclusion, as Herodotus reminds us through the words of King Xerxes (7.46), will soon pass from the scene.

Around the individual swirls the war, and around the war turns the world. Herodotus takes the entire earth, or what he calls the *oikeomenē*, "inhabited land," as the setting for his story and describes that setting as richly as he can. He traces its deserts, traverses its mountains, and tracks its rivers sluicing to the sea. He takes us inside its great cities and points out their marvels and monuments. Above all, he charts its many nations and tribes, and in each case supplies a little inset showing the outlines of their way of life. And when he reaches the boundaries of that *oikeomenē* he peers off into the great void beyond, trying to deduce or imagine what mysteries are yet to be uncovered. Like the painter of a medieval *mappamundi*, Herodotus surveys, in a vast, sweeping circuit, the arena that surrounds his great war and, indeed, all of human history.

Of course, an author, unlike a map painter, cannot display the earth whole; working in words rather than pictures, Herodotus proceeds region by region, taking each in turn and then showing (4.37–45) how they all fit together. As the author of this Hermes volume, I have encountered similar difficulties in trying to compass my subject, and I have of necessity split the *Histories* up into parts, devoting separate chapters to each. The resulting fragmented depiction badly needs the kind of reassembling that Herodotus performs on the world-map, but I have not found a way to achieve this. I can only urge readers of the *Histories*, and of this volume, to keep taking an extra step back from the canvas, to keep pushing their own minds toward the largeness of scope that Herodotus himself sought for his work. One can take delight in its particular themes and motifs, just as one can cherish particular episodes, but only at the level of the whole does one find where its true genius lies. Perhaps the same could be said of any great artwork, but I think it is more true of Herodotus's *Histories* than of most others.

Herodotus composed his *Histories*, quite possibly, over the course of his entire life, adding to it or reconfiguring it as his perceptions of the world evolved. Quite possibly it was the only work he ever wrote, and he included within it everything that captured his imagination. Above all, he made it long—longer, almost certainly, than anything else yet written in the world, and more than double the length of the longest Greek text that went before it. He gave it the plenitude of the treasure-house of Croesus, so that readers can bring out only a small portion of its stores each time they enter—even if, like the greedy Alcmaeon, they stuff their clothes, pack their cheeks, and even sprinkle their hair with gold dust. My goal in writing this volume, in keeping with the goal of the Hermes series generally, is to inspire them to keep going back in for more.

HERODOTUS

I INTRODUCTION:
MYTH AND HISTORY

I have seen editions of the *Histories* with a sculpted portrait on the cover. Some statue found in a French museum. But I never imagine Herodotus this way. I see
him more as one of those spare men of the desert who
travel from oasis to oasis, trading legends as if it is the
exchange of seeds, consuming everything without suspicion, piecing together a mirage. "This history of
mine," Herodotus says, "has from the beginning sought
out the supplementary to the main argument." What
you find in him are cul-de-sacs within the sweep of history—how people betray each other for the sake of nations, how people fall in love . . .
            —Michael Ondaatje, *The English Patient*

WHEN CROESUS, KING OF LYDIA, CLIMBED ATOP HIS FUNERAL
pyre in 547 B.C. and quite possibly immolated himself, he could
not have expected that thousands of years later anyone would
know of his demise. His kingdom in western Anatolia had
failed in its bid to become an imperial power, and its time on
the world's stage had been brief, about a century. Indeed,
Croesus may well have wished at that moment that the world
would forget him: his grandest undertaking, an invasion of the
Persian empire to the east, had ended in humiliation when the
Persians counterinvaded and caught him by surprise. He could
scarcely have imagined that, to the west, his Greek neighbors
were observing his fate and that in their retellings it would be

transformed into a downfall of tragic dimensions. Neither could he have dreamed that we in the twentieth century would regard the lighting of his pyre as one of the most emotional and significant moments in all ancient history—or rather, in the *mythic* history of the ancient world, the peculiar creation bequeathed to us by Herodotus of Halicarnassus.

Modern historians do not know what *really* happened to Croesus after his defeat by the Persians. The evidence of sixth-century sources is inconclusive, and the best research has produced only a supposition that Croesus died in the burning ruin of his palace, either by his own hand or that of Cyrus, his conqueror. We do know, however, that within decades of his death the Greeks had grown intensely interested in the fate of the king who had paid so dearly for his colossal ambitions. In fact, the image of Croesus sitting atop his funeral pyre appears on a vase by the painter Myson, the first historical subject we know of to be used in this medium (tales of gods and heroes were the norm). The downfall of a wealthy and powerful individual was to the fifth-century Greeks a gripping spectacle, as it still is to us today, but Croesus's story had an especially compelling twist: while in his prime the Lydian king had made lavish dedications at the shrines of the Greek oracles, and his generosity toward the gods had seemed to deserve a better reward. The poet Bacchylides, for one, solved this dilemma in an ode written in 468 B.C., retelling the story of Croesus on the pyre but giving it a happy ending: just before the flames reached him, Croesus was spirited off by Apollo and sent to live forever in the fairy-tale land of the Hyperboreans. Thus did Apollo remember Croesus's costly offerings at Delphi, the material symbols of his devotion to the god.

When Herodotus came to write his *Histories* more than a century after Croesus's fall, many such stories had been told about the pious man who tried for the world and lost; indeed,

Croesus's death may even have been staged as tragic drama (a vase from the mid–fifth century, unfortunately broken, seems to depict a scene from such a tragedy). But probably none of those stories approached the richness and complexity of Herodotus's account of Croesus, the first *logos*, or tale, of the *Histories*. In Herodotus's retelling, the pyre scene culminates a long process of moral education that begins early in Croesus's reign, when the Athenian sage Solon belittles the Lydian's great wealth and power. Croesus's pride is not humbled, however, either by that lesson or by the subsequent death of his beloved son Atys; only after his defeat by Cyrus and the loss of his empire, when the flames of his pyre begin to engulf him, does he understand the wisdom of Solon's words and cry out with remorse. At this moment of deep humility the pyre is miraculously quenched by a rainstorm sent by Apollo, and Croesus descends from it a sadder but wiser man. He will go on, in Herodotus's account, to become advisor to his new master, Cyrus, and to demonstrate on several occasions that (as he says himself) his sufferings have been transformed into lessons; and later still he will accompany Cyrus's deranged son Cambyses on an invasion of Egypt, serving as the sole voice of sanity and restraint at the court of a mad monarch.

Such are the metamorphic powers of mythic history: the pyre of Croesus has here become the light of an epiphany, illuminating the ethical and theological truths embodied in the rise and fall of a great man. As a result, an obscure Anatolian king of the mid–sixth century is no longer obscure; we can experience his agony and his transformation, what the Greeks would call his *pathos*, as vividly as we do those of Oedipus or Job. And to be moved by Croesus's fate is to be drawn into the vibrant tapestry of Herodotus's *Histories*, where one soon finds reasons to take an interest in persons even less noteworthy and in events even more remote from our own experience than

Croesus and his pyre of 547 B.C. It is to enter a past world in which events have meaning not merely because they occurred, but because they have been assembled, and in some cases transformed, by a writer of enormous wit, imagination, and moral intelligence.

But even as they enter this rich, meaning-laden world, readers of the *Histories* may hear a still, small voice asking from outside its portals: Is this what really happened? After all, Croesus was a real person, not a mythic hero like Oedipus. How much did Herodotus get right in describing his fall, and where did he get his information? Was there really a pyre scene like the one Herodotus describes, and if so, what was its outcome—assuming that no divinities intervened to save Croesus's life? And from what source did Herodotus learn the improbable episodes of Croesus's later career, after the descent from the pyre; or did he invent them, emboldened by the fact that no one in the Greek world knew for certain what had finally become of the Lydian king? We late-twentieth-century readers, brought up from an early age to seek out facts in the record of the past, pose such questions almost by reflex. We bristle when a modern-day historian, for example, muddies this factual record by inventing scenes or imagining dialogue, and we demand a strict redrawing of the boundary line between what really happened and the author's reconstructions or inventions.

Herodotus, too, was aware of this boundary line, which in his language divides that which can be known *atrekeōs*, truthfully or with certainty, from that which cannot. In spatial terms this line separates regions of the earth that have been seen or explored from those about which only wild rumors are told. In terms of time, moreover, Herodotus on several occasions distinguishes a historical age, the period still known through the living memory of humankind, from the age of myth enshrined in epic poems and tragic dramas, what we might today call prehistory. At the outset of the *Histories,* for example, Herodotus marks out the boundary between these two eras as he attempts to find the origin of his major geopolitical theme, the enmity between East and West. Stories told by the Persians trace this enmity to a series of legendary rapes going back to the Trojan War and even earlier, but Herodotus declines comment on this material. Instead, he says, with deliberate emphasis, "I will begin my account with the man who *I* know began unjust deeds against the Greeks," namely, Croesus of Lydia. Croesus, after all, had lived as recently as Herodotus's great-grandfather, and reliable stories about him were still in circulation; but Medea and Helen of Troy antedated him by hundreds of years, and not even the Greeks' tales about them could be verified—to say nothing of those of the Persians. Out of such distinctions, which Herodotus may well have been the first Greek writer to widely enforce, our modern, scientific approach to the past was born.

But Herodotus's temporal boundary between the ages of myth and history is in fact a fuzzier, less distinct line than appears at first glance. After all, even the poets' tales of the Trojan War contain some historical truth, as Herodotus himself implicitly acknowledges when he relies on them here and there for odd bits of information. And, as we have seen, the record of the past does not become clear when one reaches the time of Croesus, about whose life and death different stories were told. What Herodotus—or any explorer of the past— seems to be working with is actually a spectrum or sliding scale of certainty rather than a dividing line: the truth becomes gradually more recoverable as one nears the present and recedes gradually into fable as one moves backward in time. At one end of this spectrum lies the realm of myth, from which a certain amount of historical information can be extracted; at the other end lies historical reality, though even here one finds that mythic beliefs have affected the way events are remembered. At a certain point on this spectrum—about three generations before his time, as it happens—Herodotus senses that the balance between myth and history has shifted dramatically, and he imposes a boundary between the two. But his division seems arbitrary given that his own narrative becomes increasingly more accurate over its eight decades and still reveals the influence of subjective opinion and imagination even in its latest stages.

Most ancient historians, beginning in the generation after Herodotus, solved the problem of the knowability of the past by writing only about events they themselves had lived through. Moreover, when these later historians did look backward in time, they could rely on a wealth of documentary evidence for their information. Herodotus alone explored an era well before his own birth, *and* did so, for the most part, without the aid of written sources. The project earned him the scorn of Thucydides, for one, who claimed that such investigations produce only fanciful tales for the delight of an undiscriminating public. But we might also see Herodotus's undertaking in a more generous light: as an embrace of the idea that the way events are remembered and retold produces a valid kind of understanding, even when it obscures or distorts some of the facts. Herodotus, that is, had no access to the past other than through the stories he had been told, but he made a virtue of necessity and allowed those stories to lend shape and meaning to his narrative—just as poets like Bacchylides and vase painters like Myson had done.

In the spirit of this mythic history, I do not, in this Hermes volume, encourage readers to ask what really happened, at least not on a first reading of the *Histories*. In most cases their understanding and enjoyment of the text will not be diminished (and in fact may be heightened) if they read an edition that lacks historical footnotes or otherwise ignore modern, fact-oriented treatments of the archaic period. The readers' position, I believe, is like that of an audience at a film that is "based on a true story": If the movie succeeds, they will not *need* to know how much liberty was taken with the facts or what became of the characters in the end (though their curiosity may later impel them to seek out this information). Although I have included in this book two short chapters dealing with the "true story" on which the *Histories* is based, these aim only at smoothing the reader's path by providing essential background, not at showing where Herodotus got things right or wrong or at making the events themselves the main point to which the author's narrative is subordinate. And I have not dealt at all with questions of the identity or reliability of Herodotus's sources—questions that, for those readers of the *Histories* concerned with establishing an accurate record of the past, would certainly be central.

Related to the question, What *really* happened? is another issue that presses hard on some modern scholars: the trustworthiness of Herodotus when he names his sources of information or specifies the extent of his personal knowledge. In the past quarter century several writers have accused Herodotus not merely of trusting too much in others' tales but of inventing them himself and faking the attributions, of claiming to have gone places he never went, of putting his own thoughts and ideas into the mouths of his characters, and of generally behaving not just like a modern-day fiction writer but like a literary hoaxer. If such points could be proven, they would force us to read the *Histories* in a radically new way, but many of them do not seem subject either to proof or to refutation. For instance, how can we tell, when Herodotus claims to have seen an inscription on the Great Pyramid of Cheops (where, as we now know, there was none), whether he misinterpreted something he actually saw or whether he lied about having visited Egypt and in fact made up what he liked? As in all assessments of veraciousness, much depends on our intuitive judgments about the character of the author, the fallibility of memory and perception, the likelihood of detection, and other unquantifiable factors. A large majority of scholars, among whom I include myself, are inclined to take Herodotus at his word, even if that leaves a few puzzling inconsistencies between what he says and what he must have seen. Indeed, those who investigate his information thoroughly (as I cannot do in this book) often find themselves amazed at how much he gets *right.*

Again in keeping with the spirit of mythic history, I have tried to avoid calling Herodotus a historian, even though the term usually provokes no objection when applied to him by scholars. History may be his subject matter, but his approach to that subject differs from that of historians as we know them. Barbara Tuchman responded to the label "historian" by insisting that she was a journalist who happened to write about history. Using a similar distinction, we might think of Herodotus as a man of many vocations—a moralist, storyteller, dramatist, student of human nature, perhaps even a journalist himself— who found scope for all his interests in a series of events beginning with the fall of Croesus and ending, about eighty years later, with the Greek defeat of Xerxes' invasion. In truth there is no good English term to describe Herodotus's literary role in the *Histories.* John Herington, the founding editor of the Hermes series, has captured this undefinability by comparing Herodotus to a centaur: "The human forepart of the animal . . . is the urbane and responsible classical historian; the body indissolubly united to it is something out of the faraway mountains, out of an older, freer and wilder realm where our conventions have no force." No doubt this comparison would have pleased Herodotus, who has such great admiration for unconventional things from faraway lands.

Just as we must acknowledge the inadequacy of the term "historian" when applied to Herodotus, so we should recognize that his text, when published as the *History* or *Histories*, is misleadingly titled. In fact, modern translators of the text face an interesting problem when deciding what to call it. Herodotus himself never gave the work a name, the custom of literary titling not yet having evolved. When the book is first referred to by another ancient author, nearly a century after its publication—by Aristotle in his *Poetics*—it is called simply *ta Herodotou*, "the work of Herodotus." Perhaps the name *History* arose as a result of the same process that has given us *Enuma Elish*, "When above," as the title of a Babylonian creation poem: certain ancient societies routinely took the first words of a literary work as its title, and devout Jews today still refer to the Book of Genesis as *B're-sheet*, or "In the Beginning." In his opening sentence Herodotus wrote, "This is the display of the *historiē* of Herodotus of Halicarnassus," using a word that in his day denoted "research" or "inquiry" rather than a narrative of past events. The word *historiē* thus provided a convenient handle for making reference to his text, so much so in fact that the word subsequently took on a new meaning, "a work of literature based on inquiry, like that of Herodotus"—and hence started its evolution toward its modern-day meaning. (We might therefore say that Herodotus can justly be called Father of History, the honorific Cicero gave him, in at least one sense: he gave birth to the word as we now know it—he is father of "history.")

Even more misleading than *History* or *Histories* is the title *The Persian Wars*, which at least one modern publisher has applied to the work. If one were to read only the last three books of the *Histories*, as many modern college students do, one might think this a fair characterization, for here Herodotus's scope narrows to the events of Xerxes' invasion of Greece in 480–479 B.C. That title, however, is much harder to apply to the first four books, in which the "older, freer and wilder" side of the Herodotean centaur prevails. I believe that those first four books set out the themes, ideas, and structures that govern the *Histories* as a whole and that the last three books cannot be understood except as a structure built on that foundation. As a result, I have, in the chapters that follow, focused on those first four books and on the "animal" rather than the "human" aspects of the centaur, especially since readers often have difficulty with these—indeed, some hurry through them or pass them by altogether to get to the more familiar ground of *The Persian Wars*.

In printed editions and translations, the title of Herodotus's text has mostly remained, both out of respect for tradition and a lack of viable alternatives, *History* or *Histories,* and there is no changing it now (although we can understand it better if we keep in the back of our minds the phrase "natural history," in which the original meaning of Herodotus's *historiē,* an inquiry or gathering of information, survives). In times past, however, one other attempt was made at titling Herodotus's text, and that version speaks to the distance between the contents of the text and modern expectations for historical narrative. Under the Roman empire it became fashionable to refer to the nine books into which Herodotus's work had become divided as "The Muses," of whom there were also nine, and even to assign the name of a Muse to each book—a sentimental conceit, yet one that became popular in the Renaissance and survived into recent times (Rawlinson's famous English translation, standard until the mid–twentieth century, retains the names of the Muses as its titles for the nine books). No one would wish to return to "The Muses" as a title today, but the fact that it caught on to begin with is telling, reminding us that, though he took real life as his subject, Herodotus was an artist, not a documentary photographer. He was fortunate enough to live at a time when Clio, the Muse of History, consorted more often with her sisters, the Muses of Epic Poetry, Hymn, and Drama, than with the museless consorts who cluster round her today: Sociology, Economics, Political Science.

Aristotle, in the *Poetics* passage referred to above, takes some trouble to classify Herodotus's work as history, not poetry, claiming that its genre would not change even if it were put into verse. Yet Aristotle never, in any of his writings, refers to Herodotus himself as a historian. Instead, in one of his biological treatises, he calls him a *mythologos,* or "tale-teller," a type of writer whom Plato, in the *Republic,* associates so closely with the poet as to make the two indistinguishable. Thus in Aristotle's separate discussions of Herodotus, the first attempts we know of to classify him or his text, the problem posed by the *Histories* is already fully felt, as it continues to be felt today. Our modern-day libraries, bookstores, and newspaper bestseller lists ask us to define works of literature, first and foremost, as either fiction or nonfiction, yet Herodotus's work bridges even these vast, Manichaean classifications. It is a work that compasses fiction and nonfiction, myth and history, and even, to some degree, poetry and prose. Any attempt to pry apart these fused elements, to separate the two halves of the centaur, ends up diminishing its greatness and robbing us of its pleasures.

II FROM HOMER TO HERODOTUS

HERODOTUS GUESSED THAT HOMER HAD LIVED ABOUT FOUR hundred years before his own time, and he was not far wrong: the best modern estimates would shorten this span by a century or slightly more, putting Homer's life at the end of the eighth century B.C. and Herodotus's from about 485 to about 425. In those three hundred or so years, no Greek writer had attempted a narrative work of nearly the same length or scope as the Homeric epics. The *Iliad* and the *Odyssey* stood on the literary horizon like the Pillars of Heracles, the twin rock formations astride the Straits of Gibraltar: none dared pass, or even approach, those massive monuments of epic composition. During the archaic age of Greece, roughly from the early seventh century B.C. to the early fifth, the career options for epic poets were few. One could become a rhapsode and recite the Homeric epics from memory or else, like Hesiod and the authors of the Homeric hymns, create vastly shorter compositions using Homer's language and style. For the most part, poets of this period avoided epic altogether and turned their talents to lyric songs, producing a body of work that is a marvel in its own right. Homer, it seemed, had already perfected the art of long verse narrative and had left the Greeks at the end of a literary tradition when they were only just learning to write.

The three centuries separating Homer and Herodotus form about the same span of time that separates us from John Milton, author of the last long verse epic that is still widely read (even if mainly by college students). Although narrative poetry of shorter length and smaller scope continues to be written—Derek Walcott's poem *Omeros* is a notable recent example—it is hard to imagine a new epic poem on the scale of *Paradise Lost* appearing in our times; we have, however, in our own century seen a *novel* proclaim itself an epic in both its title and its thematic grandeur, James Joyce's *Ulysses*. It fell to the genius of Joyce to discover that the epic tradition could be revivified if it made the crucial transition from verse to prose, with a corresponding descent from the lofty realm of heroic myth to the more ordinary realities of mortal life. Herodotus, in his day, made a similar discovery. Though he may not have consciously aimed at creating an epic in prose, as Joyce did, he nevertheless fashioned something that was as unique for its time as *Ulysses* is for ours: a prose narrative that equaled the scope and grandeur of a Homeric poem and indeed nearly doubled the *Iliad* in sheer length.

To understand the revolutionary nature of Herodotus's achievement, it is important to recognize the paltry status of prose in Greece up until his time. Ever since the Greeks had adapted the Phoenician alphabet for their own use, in the late eighth century, they had set down all their most lofty and enduring thoughts in verse. Poetry, or *poiēsis* in Greek, was synonymous with creation, being derived from the verb *poieō*, meaning "make, form." By contrast there was for a long time no Greek term to denote prose, until finally in the fourth century we find it referred to as *psilos logos*, "naked language" (lacking the decorous "clothing" supplied by meter), or as *pedzos logos*, "language that walks on foot" (as opposed to riding in poetry's winged chariot). That is, when prose finally comes to be defined as a literary medium, nearly four centuries after the advent of writing, it is characterized simply as the absence of poetry and therefore as a second-class or demotic form of expression (the term *pedzos*, "walking on foot," has important connotations of social class because it also refers in military parlance to "the infantry," a lower social order than the high-born cavalry). Of course, by the time these terms were coined, the Greek world had already seen writers like Thucydides and Plato transform the prose medium into a vehicle for high art. But the banality of these two terms attests to prose's humble origins; it bore the stamp of its two hundred years as society's literary handmaid, useful only for legal codes, business trans-actions, inventories of goods, and other mundane applications.

In fact, the first Greeks to put prose to any truly literary use chose the most mundane of subjects: the earth itself and the surrounding cosmos. They were natural scientists, geogra-phers, and explorers, not novelists or historians. Anaximander and Anaximenes in the mid–sixth century published prose treatises about the nature of the world and the universe be-yond it; and in the following decades another prose writer, Hecataeus, made a survey of the earth's lands and peoples that came to be called the *Periodos Gēs*, or "Trip Around the World." All three men were from the city of Miletus, the intellectual and commercial hub of the region called Ionia (what is now the central part of the western coast of Turkey along with the is-lands off its shore). During their time, Miletus had become the center of a major scientific and philosophic awakening, the Ionian enlightenment as it is now called. The main thrust of these Ionian investigations was an effort to define the true or essential nature of the earth and the cosmos, either in theoreti-cal terms, as in the case of Anaximander, or else literally and empirically like Hecataeus and another early prose writer, Scy-lax, who published a log of an exploratory voyage he made into the hinterland of Asia. These sixth-century Ionians used prose as their medium of expression because their pursuit of the truth about earth and sky often led them to reject the tales told by the poets, in particular by the all-powerful Homer. Verse itself began, around this time, to seem mendacious and unreliable to some Greek thinkers; "Poets tell many lies" was a proverb already old by Aristotle's time (an idea that survives in the modern phrase "poetic license"). By contrast the "naked language" of prose, while lacking poetry's beautiful ornaments, could capture the "bare" facts about nature and about humanity. Thus another Ionian prose work, Hecataeus's *Genealogies* (so called because it traced the lineages of prominent Greek families), opened with the following declaration: "I write what I believe to be the truth, for the Greeks tell many stories which, it seems to me, are absurd." These words, with their unmistakable attack on Homer and the bardic tradition, nicely capture the spirit of the Ionian enlightenment, the movement that first developed prose as a literary medium in opposition to poetic "lies."

Other than these Ionian thinkers, there was perhaps one other figure writing Greek prose in the sixth century B.C., or at least telling stories that others soon wrote down: Aesop, whose name became synonymous with animal fable both in Greek antiquity and in recent times. Unlike his Ionian contemporaries, Aesop—supposedly a non-Greek, perhaps from Thrace or Phrygia, who entered the Greek world as a slave—used prose simply to tell stories, just as any fiction writer does today. But his stories were always of a particular type, forsaking gods and heroes for a folktale world of talking animals and embodying the practical wisdom of the low social order to which he himself supposedly belonged. In its first known application to the art of narrative, that is, Greek prose once again reveals its humble origins. Many centuries later, ancient writers would put Aesop's tales into verse in an attempt to gentrify them, but in their original form they ranked every bit as low, on a scale of both aesthetic and class status, as Homer was high. In fact, their whimsical spirit is not only un-Homeric but un-Greek, as attested by the legends of Aesop's Anatolian birth: Asiatic peoples were always more at ease with light, bawdy, fantastic tales than the comparatively prudish Hellenes, and Aesop may have been the first in a long line of outsiders who repackaged foreign traditions to suit a Greek audience.

Such, then, were the genres of prose literature we know to have preceded Herodotus: Ionian treatises on the earth and heavens and witty, low-caste Aesopic tales about the animal kingdom. Herodotus clearly learned from both, and indeed, he refers to both Hecataeus and Aesop by name in his *Histories*, where he calls them both *logopoioi*—a word by which he seems to mean, as Plato later does, "writers of prose." But his principal concern was not with either the cosmic or the animal realm, but with humanity, especially the human qualities revealed in the great events of history; and in this arena there was nothing any previous prose writer could teach him. Rather, it was Homer, and to some extent also the tragic poets of Herodotus's own day, who had plumbed the depths of human nature, who had brought characters to life by giving them speeches as well as unspoken thoughts and emotions, and who had explored the differences between human types. It was to these poets Herodotus looked when he framed his own characters in prose, and in particular when he composed the many speeches, dialogues, and conversations by which these characters are revealed.

Moreover, when Herodotus decided to make his *Histories* a long work, covering vast stretches of time and space—a decision that may have come well after he began to write, as we shall see—he again looked to Homer rather than to his prose forerunners for his model. The treatises of Hecataeus and his fellow Ionians, after all, were probably little more than pamphlets as compared with the length of what Herodotus was to create, and the fables of Aesop, at least in the form they were later recorded, were shorter still. More important, neither genre required more than the most elemental narrative techniques: Hecataeus, for his part, merely listed his information as though writing a catalogue, while Aesop in his fables rarely encountered even such minor complications as a change of scene. Herodotus found no blueprint here for his own undertaking, any more than a composer could chart out a grand opera by listening to simple folk ballads. Instead, the *Iliad* and *Odyssey* taught him how a complex tale could be organized, how action could be staged in several different places at once, how secondary or digressive material could be added to the main thread of the narrative, how a vast tale could be begun and ended. Herodotus took his structure, in other words, from Homeric epic; it was not just the best model for what he hoped to achieve, but the only one.

Finally, though the point hardly needs stressing, Herodotus's tale, like Homer's in the *Iliad* and *Odyssey*, is a record of what had happened in the past. Before Herodotus came along, the past was a realm explored only by poets; prose writers dwelt either in the eternal present of earth science and exploration or in the timeless world of Aesopic fable. Perhaps Hecataeus had begun to break through this time barrier in his *Genealogies*, which looked back to the distant past to find the ancestors of contemporary Greek families. But Herodotus went a quantum leap further, taking the past itself as his subject, just as Homer had done in the *Iliad* (a work that was regarded throughout Greek antiquity as the record of a historical Trojan War). The *Iliad* was in this regard, too, the best model available when Herodotus undertook his vast project; and the fact that the era of the *Iliad*, like that of the *Histories*, was defined by a great war between East and West only made it that much more apropos.

The idea of using prose narrative rather than verse to re-count the past had occurred to others, too, at around the same time that Herodotus composed the *Histories*. We hear of various fifth-century authors, among them Hellanicus and Damastes, who were writing regional histories—"About Egypt," "About Babylon" and the like; and though these works seem to have been mostly descriptive in character, they also included some historical narrative. Also around Herodotus's time, a Lydian named Xanthus, who wrote in Greek, produced a lurid and sensational history of his country, a work that also, to judge by the few fragments that survive, contained speeches and dia-logue. One ancient critic claims that Xanthus's writings pre-ceded Herodotus and gave him his "starting point" for the *Histories;* Herodotus himself gives no indication that he knew the work of Xanthus or his other contemporaries, and modern scholars cannot say for certain who preceded whom. In any case, it is clear that none of Herodotus's fellow *logopoioi,* or *logographoi* as they later became known, gave him more of a "starting point" than did Homer. Circumscribed in scope and in size, their treatises were only tentative forays into a new lit-erary realm, whereas Herodotus's work was a voyage of dis-covery on the order of Columbus's crossing of the Atlantic: an experiment on a monumental scale, the adaptation of the form and magnitude of Homeric poetry to the new and as-yet hum-ble craft of prose narrative.

Like Columbus, moreover, Herodotus seems not always to have known quite where he was as he plied these unfamiliar waters. His writing has none of the polished adeptness of Thucydides, who perhaps only two decades after Herodotus's death advanced the art of prose writing to ripe maturity. In his many first-person intrusions into the narrative, our author ad-mits to his frustration when he cannot obtain clear or unbiased information; he shows impatience when his own digressions or flashbacks threaten to obscure the main plot line; he labors at stage-managing his huge cast of characters and keeping his time sequence clear. Oddly enough, though, it is this very lack of polish that wins the affection of readers in a way Thucydides and later prose artists seldom do; we enjoy Herodotus's rough edges, just as, even amid the technical virtuosity of modern photography, we continue to enjoy the soft, sepia-toned look of the first albumen or platinum prints. An art form in its infancy often conveys an innocence and candor that sustains it even in later ages marked by sophistication and irony. Fortunately, in the case of Herodotus, this innocence in the realm of technique is coupled with a mature and masterful vision of what the completed work was to contain and what shape it would assume.

The suggestion that Herodotus saw the Homeric epic as his primary model is borne out by his very first sentence, which seems to evoke the *Iliad* quite deliberately. The sentence contains several words that are notoriously difficult to translate, but a fairly literal version might run as follows: "This is the setting-forth of the research of Herodotus of Halicarnassus, so that the things arising from humankind may not be dulled by time, and that great and wondrous deeds displayed by both Greeks and barbarians may not lose their renown, as regards other things and through what cause they made war upon one another." "Lose their renown" is an approximation of Herodotus's "become *aklea*," that is, lose their *kleos*, or heroic fame. If Homer had written a statement of purpose for the *Iliad*, it, too, might have contained the phrase "to prevent the deeds of Greeks and barbarians from becoming *aklea*." In fact, the same adjective occurs in an important passage of the *Iliad*, that in which two Lycian warriors, meeting on the field of battle, acknowledge why they risk their lives in war: so that their countrymen will look upon them and say, "Not without fame [*aklees*] are the kings who rule in Lycia, and who eat the fat sheep and drink the honeyed wine; their strength is great indeed, since they fight in the first wave of Lycians" (12.317–21). The *kleos* gained in the eyes of onlookers serves to set the Homeric hero apart from other, more ordinary men; to become *aklees* in this society is to become anonymous and therefore extinct to the memory of posterity, so Homer's responsibility as the preserver of *kleos* is a weighty one. Herodotus, in his opening sentence, shoulders that same responsibility and even extends it, as he proclaims in the two parallel purpose clauses that make up the core of that sentence: he will preserve the historical record generally ("the things arising from humankind") as well as the glory of individual deeds from the erosion wrought by the passage of time.

But if the central segment of Herodotus's opening sentence reads like something Homer might have said, the clauses on either end are distinctly un-Homeric. We have already taken note of the word that comes third in the original Greek, *historie*, or "inquiry, research," and have seen how this word became both the title of the work as a whole and the name for its genre. Though it derives from a Homeric word, *histor*, meaning a judge or arbitrator, this abstract noun was unknown to Homer and the other epic bards, who, because they received their stories from an all-knowing Muse, had no need to make an "inquiry" about anything contained therein. By labeling his work a "setting-forth of *historie*," therefore, Herodotus signals his break from the epic tradition almost as decisively as he does by using prose as a medium rather than verse. No longer can the Muse be invoked as a guarantor of authenticity; human powers of investigation and reason have been called upon to take the place of this reverend goddess. (Hecataeus's prose treatise *Genealogies*, which as we have seen opened with a sharp attack on the ridiculous stories of the bardic tradition, was also referred to in antiquity by the alternative title *Historiai*, or "researches," the same title that was applied to Herodotus's work.)

Perhaps even more remarkably un-Homeric, however, are the words that precede *historie̅* in the original Greek of this opening sentence: the author's name and place of origin, "of Herodotus of Halicarnassus." The flexibility of the Greek language's case system enabled Herodotus to place these two words anywhere he wished, so their initial position makes an emphatic statement of authorship—a kind of statement routine for modern-day writers, who always affix their names to their titles, but still quite unusual in fifth-century Greece. Homer, after all, never mentions his own name in the *Iliad* or *Odyssey* and only very rarely speaks in the first-person singular. Like most poets who work within an oral tradition, he makes that tradition the source of his story, keeping his individual artistry out of the spotlight as much as possible. Herodotus, by contrast, steps forward to claim authorship of his narrative the very moment it has begun; he identifies himself, as it were in boldface type, as the sole originator of his *Histories*. Granted, he had some precedent for this move: some decades earlier, Hecataeus had opened his *Genealogies* with a similar self-proclamation, "Hecataeus the Milesian relates what follows." But such an opening was as yet a departure from narrative traditions and signals a redefinition of the author's responsibility for his work.

If the opening three words of this first sentence, then, mark a distinct break from Homer, so too do its final phrases. Leaving aside for the moment the curiously vague reference to "other things," let us take note of Herodotus's bold decision to make not merely the conflict between East and West but the *cause* of that conflict a major theme of his investigation. For this step he had no known precedent, and in fact his use of the word translated "cause" here, *aitiē*, established a new meaning that later became standard among Greek philosophers (giving the root of our word "aetiology"). Readers of modern historiography take for granted that this "why" question will be asked in any account of a major war and that answers will be sought in underlying social, political, and economic factors. But such a question was not obvious in an age when armed conflict among nations was as normal a process as corporate competition in today's business world. Homer, for instance, had never bothered to account for the cause of the Trojan War in the *Iliad*, beyond placing Helen, the adulterous wife of the Greek king Menelaus, inside the walls of Troy with her lover Paris. But Herodotus does not accept the notion that a single face might launch a thousand ships, as he indicates in his dismissive treatment of the Persian rape-myths he catalogues in his opening chapters. Such tales, though not manifestly untrue, could not reveal the *aitiē* that Herodotus claims as part of his subject matter in his opening sentence.

Unfortunately, it is not at all clear what Herodotus *does* have in mind when he sets out on his investigation of *aitiē*. Almost certainly he does not mean, Who was to blame for starting the war? even though the word *aitiē* and related terms, in other contexts, can refer to legal or moral culpability. Approaching the sequence of events in the *Histories* as an attempt to discover who started it gets nowhere fast: Croesus, who was the first Asian ruler in Herodotus's knowledge to have harmed the Greeks, did not harm them much, and his initial subjugation of the Hellenic city-states bordering his empire does not lead to any retribution from Greece or establish a chain of cause and effect. (Later, Xerxes, in his speech announcing a Persian attack on Greece, further confounds the idea of a retributive scheme of justice in the *Histories* by promising to enslave both *aitioi* and *anaitioi*, those who have harmed the Per-

sians and those who have not [7.8].) Neither is it easy to believe
that Herodotus is here asking, What motivated the Persians to
mount their invasions of the Greek mainland? for that question
receives no single or definitive answer within the text. The author himself makes no explicit statement on the subject, as
Thucydides, for example, does in the case of the Peloponnesian
War ("I believe the truest reason . . . is that the rise of Athens to
greatness incited fear in the Spartans and compelled them to
fight," 1.23). Rather, he displays a multitude of incentives in
the speeches, conversations, and thoughts of his characters,
ranging from Queen Atossa's desire for Greek serving maids
(3.134), to Mardonius's anger against Athens for having aided
the Ionian revolt (7.9), to the several competing goals advanced
by Xerxes: acquisition of fertile land, winning of personal
glory, even (improbably enough) a preemptive strike against
power-hungry Greeks who might otherwise conquer Asia (7.8,
11). All of these qualify as factors contributing to the conflict or
as individual and idiosyncratic understandings of it, but none
seems to answer the question in the form Herodotus states it,
"through what *aitiē* they made war on one another."

  To some degree this *aitiē* does not bear explanation because,
as one Herodotean scholar has recently shown, its principal
component is the imperialist impulse by which the Persians attack everyone in their path; the Greeks simply took their turn,
after most of Asia and North Africa had already been absorbed. In the closing sentences of the *Histories*, in fact, Herodotus tells how the Persians had chosen, in the time of their first
ruler, Cyrus, to live in a tough country and rule others, rather
than move to a soft land and be ruled. This initial decision
seems to have set them on the road to their entire subsequent
history, with its restlessness, militarism, and continual expansion. So what Herodotus really needs to explain is not so much
the cause but the *roots* of the Greco-Persian wars, that is, how

they got to the point that they reached. His opening question about *aitiē* is answered not by a Thucydides-style analysis but by his own choice of a starting point for the narrative: the moment at which Asian imperialism, in its relentless quest for new territory, first encroached upon the outer fringe of the Greek world. After much contemplation of the Persian Wars, Herodotus must have decided that only by going back to that point, some eighty years before the end of the conflict, could he put subsequent events into their proper context. Thus he ends his opening sentence with a clause, "through what cause they warred with one another," that steers his readers to his chosen starting point—just as Homer's final lines in the opening of the *Iliad*, "from the time when Agamemnon and Achilles first quarreled in strife," plunk us down at the opening of that poem's narrative.

I say "after much contemplation" because Herodotus seems to have chosen this starting point relatively late in the game, after he had already written what are now books 7 through 9 of the *Histories*—a segment sometimes referred to as the Xerxiad because they tell the story of King Xerxes' expedition into Greece. The question of whether the *Histories* was composed in pieces is a sticky one and will be dealt with more fully in the next chapter. For now let us say that even if Herodotus arrived in midstream at his plan to give accounts of Croesus, Cyrus, Cambyses, and Darius before reaching that of Xerxes, that plan is no less a thing of genius, an essential aspect of what I have here described as his epic ambition. Homer, after all, had similarly decided that the fate of Achilles could not stand alone as the story of the *Iliad*. In fact, he takes his main character off the scene for much of the poem while he gives prominent episodes to other heroes, creating, as it were, a gallery of human portraits; when Achilles then returns to battle, we can situate his portrait within this gallery and perceive his character in all its brilliant definition. And if this were not a broad enough context, Homer goes yet further: at the moment of this return he pauses to describe Achilles' god-given shield, with its scenes of war, harvest, marriage, and all the other activities of the world that surrounds the epic hero. Herodotus creates a similarly broad array of human types in the *Histories* but arranges them sequentially rather than en masse, since his "heroes," the rulers of Lydia and Persia and the leaders of various Greek states, succeed one another over the course of three or four generations. Nevertheless, they are all present to our minds at the end of the story because Herodotus reminds us, either in his own words or in those he assigns to his characters, of how Xerxes' actions compare with those of his predecessors. Like Homer, that is, Herodotus examines the problems of warfare and rule by assembling a series of representative types; but his portrait gallery, unlike Homer's, spreads out across a corridor of time.

And not only time, but also space; for just as Homer had used the shield of Achilles to extend his poem's ambit to the shores of Ocean, so Herodotus takes the entire world as the backdrop of the *Histories*. During the eighty years of its imperial history, Persia had either invaded or subjugated most of western and central Asia as well as parts of Europe and Africa. By following the course of these actual or attempted conquests in his first five books, Herodotus conducts an intermittent "Trip Around the World," similar in its comprehensiveness to that of Hecataeus but more far-reaching in its level of detail. Indeed, his intention seems to have been to provide in the *Histories* descriptions of every tribe and nation about whom anything could be learned, so that he also includes sketches of peoples in the hinterlands of northern Europe and West Africa whom the Persians had not attacked. These ethnographies, as they are called—some as short as a sentence, others occupying many pages—contribute to the breadth and expansiveness of the *Histories* and form a major part of its inquiry into the human condition.

These thoughts call our attention back to the opening sentence of the *Histories* and in particular to the one phrase I have not yet dealt with, the fuzzy "as regards other things" in its ultimate clause. This phrase must have been made vague by intention, seeing that the entire sentence has been crafted with consummate care. It is as if Herodotus were leaving a vast loophole in his statement of purpose, saying, in effect, "I reserve the right to include in this work anything that seems interesting, whether or not it is directly relevant to my main theme." Thus tribes outside the sphere of Persian influence are fair game, as are accounts of plants and animals, geography and geology, marvels and miracles, lore and legend. In a famous aside to his audience, Herodotus tells us that his story "has from the start sought out" digressions, as though these were both a natural and desirable aspect of his genre (4.30). For a narrative of such inclusiveness and elasticity, his best model was, once again, Homer's *Iliad*—a work that includes within its ambit, as its title proclaims, any and all "things concerning Troy."

Of course, there is one major area in which Herodotus could not follow Homer's example, an area that indeed makes the very notion of a prose epic seem a contradiction in terms. In the *Iliad,* the battle around the city of Troy is interrupted by scenes set among the gods on Olympus, and these gods can also intervene in the battle either in disguise or in their divine forms. The same is true in the *Odyssey,* although generally speaking the gods have less of a presence in that poem. In any case, divine intervention in human affairs had been established as an indispensable part of the machinery of Greek epic; and

when the Romans later learned the craft of epic poetry from the Greeks, they employed the same machinery, save for the sole (and not very successful) experiment of Lucan's *Pharsalia*. After a first glance at Herodotus's *Histories* we might be tempted to say that it bears no comparison to Homer in this crucial aspect; it contains, after all, no colloquies of the gods, and it does not show divinities descending from Olympus to take part in the action below. But that is not to say that the gods are not present and active in the events of the *Histories*. Herodotus in fact surrounds his narrative with divine interventions at every turn, though in his case they are of the indirect variety: oracles, dreams, portents, miraculous storms, and other apparitions that in most cases are unmistakably sent by the gods as part of their governance of humankind. Herodotus's characters, in other words, stands in relation to their Homeric counterparts as the Hebrew prophets to the patriarchs: although they may not meet with deity face to face, they are aware of its presence and see the divine will expressed everywhere around them.

In fact, it is in his use of dreams, oracles, and prophecies to explain human behavior that Herodotus often closely resembles Homer, especially because the oracles he quotes within his text are usually poems in the Homeric meter, dactylic hexameter. There are more than two dozen of these verse interludes scattered throughout the *Histories*, and they are more frequent in the first book than in any of the others; seven come in a dense cluster between chapters 47 and 85, in the story of Croesus and the accounts of sixth-century Athens and Sparta. We might therefore infer that Herodotus indulges his interest in oracles and prophecies more freely at the earliest stratum of his narrative, when he deals with semilegendary events, and in this we would not be wrong. But it is also true that Herodotus uses these opening stories to set both tone and pattern for those that follow. They form a kind of prelude, helping us tune our ears to the music of the *Histories;* and thus their high concentration of hexameter quotations serves to impart some of the solemnity of epic to the narrative as a whole. James Joyce made a similar move (though in a more comic spirit) in the opening sentences of *Ulysses:* the first character to speak there intones a line of Latin from the Catholic Mass.

Apart from his quotations of verse oracles, moreover, Herodotus evokes the divine mechanisms of the Homeric cosmos at many points in his story. While he keeps the gods themselves offstage, Herodotus goes out of his way to implicate them in significant historical events. For example, Xerxes' decision to invade Greece at the beginning of book 7, arguably the most critical turning point in the entire narrative, is more than a merely human event: when Xerxes tries to change his mind and cancel the invasion, he is told by a divine figure in a dream that the attack must go ahead. This story of the dream (attributed by Herodotus to his Persian informants) bears a strong resemblance to an episode in book 2 of the *Iliad* in which Agamemnon is told in a dream to press his attack against Troy. Whether or not Herodotus was conscious of the resemblance, he clearly took pains to bring the divine into his narrative at this crucial juncture. That is, Herodotus does not wish to portray Xerxes reaching his decision merely through a mortal's political and military calculations, any more than Homer would have depicted the Greek defeat of Troy as a simple matter of superior weaponry and tactics.

Another good illustration of this point comes in the one passage in which Herodotus actually analyzes the *Iliad,* in a famous addendum to his discussion of the Helen in Egypt myth. During his investigations in the Egyptian city of Memphis, Herodotus reports, he discovered a story that Helen had not gone to Troy with her seducer Paris, as Homer had supposed, but had been detained by the pharaoh Proteus while stopping in

Egypt en route. Helen had thereafter passed ten years in Egypt while the Greeks ignorantly battered the walls of Troy, half a world away, seeking her release. Herodotus recognizes the problems this story raises for readers of the *Iliad* and states his own opinion as follows:

> If Helen had been at Troy, she would have been given back to the Greeks whether Paris was willing or not. For neither Priam [king of Troy] nor his relatives were so deranged as to wish to place their own persons, their children, and their city at risk so that Paris might live with Helen. Perhaps they felt this way at the beginning, but when many of the other Trojans were dying whenever they met the Greeks in battle, and when two, three or even more of Priam's own sons were being slain every time a battle occurred (if one must base one's discussion on the epic poets)—when such things were happening, I expect that, even if Priam himself had been living with Helen, he would have given her back to the Greeks. . . . Rather, they weren't able to give Helen back [since she wasn't there at all], and when they told the truth about this the Greeks didn't believe them; since, to express my own opinion, divinity arranged that they would be wholly destroyed and thereby make clear to humankind that great misdeeds receive great punishments from the gods. (2.120)

How far off from Homer Herodotus seems in this passage— and yet, perhaps not so far after all. Substituting a latter-day realpolitik for Homer's heroic code, Herodotus analyzes the political and military disposition of Troy in a way that is wholly out of tune with the *Iliad* (even while relying on the historical accuracy of the poem's information). But this odd chain of reasoning does not lead to the conclusion we might have expected, that Homer's account of the war is wholly fictional—a possibility already contemplated earlier in the discussion, at 2.118. Instead, Herodotus smoothes out the logical kinks he has uncovered by invoking a higher power, *to daimonion*, the vaguest possible name for the gods or the divine in general. It was this power, Herodotus supposes, that had kept the Greeks at Troy even after the Trojans had told them that Helen wasn't there—in retribution for wrongs that Herodotus does not name (and that his readers are hard-pressed to identify).

What makes this conclusion so startling is that Herodotus need not have invoked *to daimonion* at all to solve his logical problem with the *Iliad*'s plot. After all, what attacking army *would* believe a besieged enemy who told them that they wouldn't get what they came for, that they might as well turn around and go home? Herodotus's theory works perfectly well on a practical and human level but its efficacy is not enough to satisfy Herodotus. Time and again, he reveals his fundamental sense that the sphere of human life is surrounded by, watched over, and influenced by the gods or by god—Herodotus quite often uses the singular, as though he considered all deities part of a unified divine order—and any action taken within that sphere calls forth a response from that which lies beyond it.

In his inclusion of the divine as an indispensable element in human history, as in many of his authorial moves, Herodotus was pioneering the use of prose to tell a story as yet unattempted except in verse. Lacking the omniscience conferred on the epic poets by the Muse, Herodotus can tell us nothing of the upper world; indeed, he seems ill at ease even discussing legends of the gods in too much detail. Like the Ionian scientists and geographers from whom he inherited his medium, Herodotus concentrates on what can be learned through *historiē*, factual inquiry, or on what can be inferred on the basis of physical evidence. But even while keeping his narrative earthbound, Herodotus brings into it whatever signposts of the divine his new genre would allow. His tales of oracles, portents, and dreams are of this world, but they serve as reminders that *to daimonion*, divinity in all its diverse manifestations, is still as valid a way of understanding human affairs as were the gods of Homer some three centuries earlier.

III THE SIXTH CENTURY: THE NEW WORLD ORDER

Earlier I claimed that one need not use a historical commentary to read Herodotus for pleasure and meaning because the goal of the *Histories* is not merely to give an accurate record of events. A lack of historical background, however, *can* impede one's enjoyment of the text, if only because some of the players on Herodotus's great stage may initially be obscure and hard to sort out. Herodotus's first book, for example, presents a magnificent panorama of Near Eastern peoples and places that are often unfamiliar to modern-day readers, even those who bring to it a substantial background in Greek history. What is more, Herodotus complicates the reader's task by frequently disrupting the time sequence of his narrative and introducing long flashbacks (and on a few occasions, flash-forwards). The looseness of the text's chronological structure is especially apparent in book 1, where Herodotus opens not with the earliest of the events he records but with "the first [Asian] man I know to have begun unjust deeds against the Greeks" (1.5). Readers encountering these events for the first time may not find it easy to keep track of the sequence in which they occurred, so I have tried to restore that sequence in the following brief sketch of the period covered by the first four books of the *Histories*.

A quick survey of archaic Greek and Near Eastern history will also allow readers to take the full measure of the cataclysmic events about which Herodotus wrote. The Persian state founded by Cyrus and extended under Cambyses and Darius was an entity the ancient world had never seen: a centralized empire on a global scale, the forerunner of the even larger empires of Alexander and the Roman Caesars. Though it was to some degree anticipated by the Assyrian empire of the eighth and seventh centuries, it was vastly larger, more complex, and better organized. Its power enabled Herodotus, for one, to imagine that it was bent on adding all Europe to its already vast dominion in Asia and North Africa and therefore to conquer the entire known world—an ambition that the Greeks alone, with their comparatively tiny population and impoverished resources, were in a position to block. Thus, in Herodotus's eyes, nothing less than the fate of the planet (that is, as much of it as he knew) depended on the great battles of 480 and 479 B.C., events that form the climax of the narrative in books 7, 8 and 9.

But it is the entire life cycle of the Persian empire, not merely its ultimate retrenchment by the Greeks, that Herodotus documents. Thus he begins his narrative about eight decades before its endpoint and includes even a quick summary of events going back a century before that. He sets his scene first in Anatolia, among the Lydians, but then moves quickly into Asian territories little known to the Greeks of his day: Babylon, Assyria, Scythia, and Persia itself. The Hellenic city-states, by contrast, remain out of the action during the first half of *Histories*, except when those located on the Asian littoral become victims of larger powers. Herodotus carefully follows their development within their own region, but only in book 5, about halfway through the entire narrative, do they emerge as David-like challengers to the Goliath of Persian world rule (at which point my outline of history will resume, in chapter X).

In the middle of the sixth century, the Near East was going through rapid changes as its old, established superpowers were replaced by a new world order. In this period, the last of the great Semitic civilizations to dominate the region, Assyria, had grown too weak to sustain its hegemony; it had exhausted itself through reaching out from its central position, in northern Mesopotamia, to control its neighbors on all sides—in particular the rebellious Babylonians to the south and, much further afield, the once-great kingdom of Egypt. Thus with none of the traditional powers of the Near East able to steer its affairs, and Egypt no longer able to influence them from the outside, the stage was set for a group of peoples newly arrived on the scene. The first few centuries of the first millennium had seen large numbers of Iranian tribes (some of whom are probably the ancestors of modern-day Iranians) move westward into the region, driven by unknown pressures: the Medes and Persians had settled to the east of the Assyrian empire, and the nomadic Scythians and Sacae had later occupied the north. These newcomers as yet lacked the social organization and material wealth of the older peoples; the Medes, according to Herodotus, had only around 700 B.C. linked their scattered villages into a single nation under King Deioces, and the Scythians remained a loose aggregate of nomadic tribes centuries later. But their hardihood and mastery of horsemanship and archery made them effective warriors. The Medes had in fact joined with the Babylonians to destroy the Assyrian capital of Nineveh in 612, and thereafter the two nations had divided up Assyrian territory, the Medes occupying the northern half and Babylon the southern.

While these struggles went on at the center of the Near East, another newly risen nation was amassing power in Anatolia on its western fringe: the Lydians, who had organized into a prosperous and aggressive state under the Mermnad kings (it is with the founding of this dynasty, by Gyges, that Herodotus commences the narrative of the *Histories*, in chapter

7 of book 1). These Lydians belonged to a very different type of society from the nomadic peoples to the east; their strength lay in the rich mineral resources of their homeland rather than in the toughness of their lifestyle (a contrast driven home in a story Herodotus tells at 1.71). Their proximity to the Greek cities of the Anatolian coast had also led to their partial adoption of Hellenic ways, so it is not surprising to find the Lydian kings, especially Croesus, making elaborate offerings at the shrines of the Greek oracles. But the Lydians seem to have been just as intent as their eastern rivals, the Medes, on filling the power vacuum at the heart of the Near East. Friction between the two peoples led to an indecisive war in the 580s—its final battle can be dated to May 28, 585, thanks to Herodotus's report that a solar eclipse had ended the fighting (1.74)—after which an uneasy truce was declared and the river Halys, which nearly divides the Anatolian peninsula into eastern and western halves, was made the boundary between their domains.

The historical landscape that Herodotus surveys at the opening of the *Histories,* then, looks like this: Two rising empires, the Lydians and Medes, and one old-world power, Babylon, vie with one another for supremacy in the Near East; the Egyptians, though once great enough to dictate to any of these nations, now stand by as mere spectators to the struggle, no doubt fearing that their vast wealth would ultimately become the victor's prize. Herodotus focuses his attention first on the two new-world peoples, dealing with them by turns: the Lydians, under King Croesus, dominate the first half of book 1, up to chapter 95; after that the narrative moves eastward to the Medes and to Cyrus, the Persian leader who seizes Median power and founds the dynasty that will lead it to greatness. (The two halves of book 1 thus cover different, but overlapping, time periods in different parts of the world: the first follows Croesus from his accession in 560 to his defeat in 546, the

second follows Cyrus from his birth around 585 to his death in
529.) Another nation of newcomers, the northerly Scythians,
also puts in brief appearances in both halves of book 1: Herodotus refers at several points to a violent southward invasion
they had made in pursuit of their mysterious foes, the Cimme-
rians, and to their resulting twenty-eight-year period of domination in western Asia (e.g., 1.103–6). Although the Medes had
finally succeeded in chasing them back beyond the Caucasus
mountains, the Scythians remained a threat to the northern
frontier of the Near East, such that the Persians would later
launch a full-scale invasion of their territory (an episode Herodotus relates in close detail in book 4.)

Like the Lydians and Medes, the Greeks were a part of the
new world order in the sixth century, having only recently
emerged from a long period of disorganization and coalesced
into the units that would define their culture forever after,
poleis, or city-states. Of these, Sparta was indisputably the most
powerful and best able to project its power abroad. All the
Greek city-states had, by the mid–sixth century, developed a
style of warfare using heavily-armed soldiers known as hoplites, standing together in close formations, but the Spartans
had perfected the technique; indeed, they had organized their
entire society as a vast boot camp for hoplites, and Spartan
males spent almost their whole lives in military training or service. As a result, a Spartan hoplite force could defeat even a far
more numerous enemy; constant drill prepared them to stay in
formation and execute complex maneuvers even in the heat of
battle. Other Greek cities, including Athens, did not adopt an
extensive system of military training like Sparta's but relied on
adult males to take the field when needed, bringing their own
armor with them. In their case, power was based on the size
and cohesion of the citizen body, in particular on the number
of men wealthy enough to afford shields and armor, and in

these categories Athens perhaps held a slight lead over the other states. Athens and Sparta, then, had emerged as the leading powers of the rapidly developing Greek world, as Herodotus makes clear in book 1 when he digresses from Lydian history to introduce these two major Greek players (chapters 56–70). But Athens was very much second in importance to Sparta, and both were vastly smaller and weaker than any of the Asian peoples who are Herodotus's principal concern in this first book.

The weakness and disunity of the Hellenic city-states, along with the wealth they generated through industry and trade, made them inviting prey for the rising powers of the Near East. For those Greeks fortunate enough to live on islands, the sea provided a guarantee of freedom: the Hellenes had mastered the art of seamanship early on, and their navies were a match for any potential invader, as Herodotus makes clear in a little parable at 1.27. (The Phoenicians, who had also become expert sailors at an early stage, had little interest in fighting the Aegean Greeks, until the Persians later compelled them to do so.) And with land travel between Europe and Asia cut off by the Black Sea and Bosporus, the Greeks of the European mainland were, until the fifth century at least, left alone to war among themselves. But the Greeks who had settled on the coast of Turkey lacked these safeguards and so became targets of Asian imperialism starting in the seventh century. First, Gyges of Lydia attacked three Ionian cities, as Herodotus tells us at 1.15, and captured one of them; when his great-great-grandson Croesus came to power, he subdued all the coastal Greek cities and imposed tribute on them. Because he thus made a large-scale, continuing effort to subjugate these cities, Croesus was the man, according to Herodotus, who "began unjust deeds against the Greeks," though strictly speaking his ancestor Gyges had struck the first blow.

While Croesus was expanding Lydian territory in Anatolia and harvesting the region's gold deposits (thus becoming a proverbial figure for wealth, as in "rich as Croesus"), a dynamic new Persian leader, Cyrus, was consolidating power in the Median empire beyond the Halys river. Readers of the *Histories* should not be confused if the names Mede and Persian, virtually synonymous elsewhere in Greek literature and in biblical texts, here designate two separate peoples. Ethnically the Medes and Persians were kin, and they had lived in close association ever since their arrival in the Near East, though the Medes had traditionally held some degree of sovereignty over the Persians. Around 550, however, Cyrus, a Persian vassal king, inverted this hierarchy by leading an uprising against his Median master, Astyages. With Cyrus now in command of the empire, the Medes and Persians became even more closely knit; in the stone reliefs that adorned the palaces of the Persian capital Persepolis, for example, Median and Persian figures stand side by side, presumably in equal honor, at the court of the Great King, distinguished only by their dress, headgear, and shoes. Even Herodotus, who speaks of the Persians in the early books of the *Histories* as though they were former slaves of the Medes, later uses the two peoples' names interchangeably, implying that after Cyrus's accession, as a Greek history professor once explained to his class, "One man's Mede is another man's Persian."

Cyrus claimed descent from an ancient heroic figure named Achaemenes, and so the dynasty he founded and the culture it produced have become known to history as Achaemenid. Incidentally, the Persian names used in this book, Cyrus, Achaemenes, and so on, are written in the Hellenized forms Herodotus gave them. In the Persian language they would look and sound quite different: Kurash, Haxaimanish.

In his new role as king of the combined nations, Cyrus controlled the vast swath of territory won by the Medes from Assyria and thus posed a new threat to Croesus's Lydian domain to the west. The moment had arrived for a major showdown between these two powers, with the overlordship of the entire Near East hinging on the outcome. Croesus prepared for the struggle by enlisting the help of the surviving old-world nations, Babylon and Egypt, and even by forming an alliance with comparatively puny Sparta (as Herodotus relates, 1.56–70, 77). But Cyrus held his own against this allied force and then turned the tables on Croesus, mounting a surprise attack on him after he had broken off fighting and returned to Lydia for the winter. In this counterinvasion Cyrus displayed the energy and tactical skills of an Alexander or a Napoleon, covering hundreds of miles of rough terrain so rapidly that "he arrived in Lydia as his own messenger," as Herodotus says (that is, he appeared before any of Croesus's scouts had time to forewarn the Lydians). Croesus was besieged in his capital, Sardis, and the city fell to the Persians before the Lydians' allies could arrive to relieve it.

Cyrus's defeat of Croesus won him the enmity of Babylon and Egypt, both because they had allied with Lydia against him and feared retribution and because their own survival as autonomous nations now clearly depended on stopping Persian expansion. Cyrus, according to Herodotus, immediately laid plans for attacks on both states as well as on the nomadic Scythian peoples who constricted his northeastern frontiers (1.153); he marched first against the Babylonians (whom Herodotus misleadingly calls Assyrians at 1.178). According to a historical record recovered from Babylon in recent times, the Babylonians were then in a state of deep civil strife, and one of their factions may well have betrayed the capital to Cyrus to gain the upper hand; Herodotus gives a different account but supports the idea that Cyrus captured Babylon without a fight— a city so vast that those dwelling in its center, as Herodotus reports with a typically tragic sense of irony, continued to dance and enjoy themselves at a feast, not realizing that the perimeter had already fallen (1.191). While this was taking place, moreover, Cyrus sent an expeditionary force under his general Harpagus to deal with the Anatolian Greeks, who had also sided with Croesus in the Lydio-Persian war, and this campaign, which resulted in the subjection of the entire coast to Cyrus, is described by Herodotus at great length (1.141–170).

In the course of only two decades, Cyrus had pushed his empire to the western and southern boundaries of Asia and had established the new world order for good. The sudden collapse of Babylon, following only two generations after the equally staggering fall of Assyria, signaled to all observers that the day of the great Semitic powers had passed and that the Persians were to be masters of the East. The momentousness of these events can be felt not only in Herodotus but in the Hebrew Bible as well: the famous "writing on the wall" of the Book of Daniel, for example, was a warning to Belshazzar, king of Babylon, that "your kingdom is divided and given to the Medes and Persians," though there the conquering general is mistakenly identified as Darius rather than Cyrus. The meaning of Babylon's fall is explored in greater depth in the later chapters of Isaiah (the portion known as Second Isaiah). Here Cyrus is hailed as the redeemer of the Jewish people, the savior who released them from a fifty-year "Babylonian captivity" and returned them to their homeland:

> Thus says the Lord to his anointed, to Cyrus,
> whose right hand I have grasped
> to subdue the nations before him

and strip kings of their robes,
to open doors before him. . . .
For the sake of my servant Jacob,
and Israel my chosen,
I call you by your name,
I surname you, though you do not know me.

(Isaiah 45.1–4)

Indeed, Cyrus is the only gentile referred to in the Bible as being "anointed," *messiah* in Hebrew; his coming had overturned the old world and liberated the Jews so suddenly that he appeared to be an unwitting instrument of God's will. Strange to tell, modern Christmas revelers continue to commemorate Cyrus, though usually without realizing it: for the composer Handel adapted parts of Second Isaiah for his *Messiah* oratorio, so that the beautiful prophecies that open that work, though seeming in their new context to celebrate the coming of Christ, were actually written in honor of Cyrus the Persian.

It was left to Cyrus's son, Cambyses, to complete his father's plans by conquering Egypt, the last of the old-world powers, after Cyrus himself had died fighting in the northeast corner of his empire (according to Herodotus, that is; other sources give different accounts of his death). Cambyses' march on Egypt gives Herodotus the opportunity for a long narrative detour, and he fills all of book 2 with the geology, social mores, biology, and political history of that miraculous land. Here, we must recall, Herodotus surveys a culture that dated as far back in time from his own day as the classical Greek world does from ours; the building of the pyramids, for example, preceded the events of the *Histories* by more than twenty centuries. But the era that saw the rise of the Persians had been for Egypt a time of foreign occupation and decline, so that by Herodotus's day this proud country was fast on its way to becoming, as it remained for another millennium, the ancient world's foremost archaeological museum. A series of invasions by the Assyrians to the north and the Nubians to the south had greatly weakened the Egyptian pharaohs, and they had begun to rely on foreign mercenaries to fight their wars for them—among these, Greek hoplites, as Herodotus relates (2.152–55). In fact, an eloquent testimony to this Greek involvement in Egyptian military affairs has come to light on one of the colossal statues of Rameses II at Abu Simbel, just north of what is now Egypt's border with Sudan. Here a band of Greek mercenaries, employed by Psammetichus II during his invasion of the Nubian lands to the south, carved their names and, in one case, a brief narrative onto the statue's leg (anticipating the "Kilroy was here" graffiti that American G.I.'s have left all over the world). Herodotus himself makes note of the expedition, assigning it to a pharaoh named Psammis (2.161), and Egyptian documents allow us to date it to 591 B.C. So Greek soldiers were already helping to prop up the Egyptian army by this date, though, as Herodotus makes clear in the later chapters of book 2, certain nationalistic Egyptians did not like to admit that things had fallen so far.

Although the strength of Egypt was gone, its wealth remained, and the annual flooding of the Nile made its soil incredibly rich and productive of grain. Cambyses thus had ample economic reasons for extending Persian dominion in this direction, apart from wanting to punish the Egyptians' support of Lydia in the war against his father Cyrus—or the neglect his mother had endured after Cyrus took up with an Egyptian mistress (a story Herodotus relates, though skeptically, at 3.3). Thus the invasion that Herodotus presents as Cambyses' personal vendetta, leading to the mistreatment of the conquered pharaoh, Psammenitus, and to a series of vicious outrages against local customs, was more likely part of a carefully planned program of imperial expansion. Enfeebled Egypt fell to Cambyses in short order, and soon thereafter the Persians also received the submission of the Greek trading cities on the North African coast, Barca and Cyrene, and the island of Cyprus.

But Cambyses also tried to conquer the more distant regions of Africa like Carthage and Ethiopia, and these expeditions, according to Herodotus, resulted in failure and in grave losses to his armies. Worse yet, Cambyses had been three years in Egypt when he heard that his brother Smerdis had seized his throne back in Persia; as he hastened back home to deal with the crisis, he met with an accident and died. According to a story later spread among the Persians and repeated by Herodotus, this usurper was not in fact Smerdis, whom Cambyses had already secretly had killed, but a member of the Magi priesthood—Gaumata is the name Persian sources give him—who had craftily assumed the identity of the royal Smerdis. According to this version of events, the impostor's identity eventually came under suspicion, and Darius, a Persian nobleman and descendant of the royal family in a collateral line, led a band of men who killed him and ended the usurpation. Modern historians have treated this "false Smerdis" story with grave skepticism, especially seeing that Darius, after occupying the throne himself, did his utmost to publicize it—even carving it in three languages onto a high cliff face at a site called Behistun, where it can still be seen. Perhaps Smerdis really was an impostor, but our modern experience of political crimes and cover-ups leads to a more cynical hypothesis: Darius invented Gaumata as a smokescreen, whereas the man he killed in seizing power was in fact Smerdis, the legitimate son of Cyrus. Probably this ancient murder mystery will never be solved to everyone's satisfaction, but the outcome of the whole confused episode is clear enough: In 522 the Persian throne passed over into a new branch of the Achaemenid family, and the line of Cyrus and Cambyses came to an end.

Darius had to move quickly to consolidate his hold on power because during the tumult surrounding his accession much of the empire had risen in revolt; Herodotus describes the reconquest of Babylon starting at 3.150, though he ignores many other, similar campaigns. (Herodotus also omits mention of Darius's important religious innovation, the introduction at the highest level of Persian society of Zoroastrianism—the monotheistic faith that survives even today in small pockets of Iran and India.) After securing control of the empire, he proceeded to reorganize it, employing a scheme that now seems obvious but that was highly original in its time: The vast realm was divided into twenty or so provinces (the number varied), which Herodotus twice calls by their Persian name, *satrapies*. An administrative capital for the whole empire was established at the ancient city of Susa, near the head of the Persian gulf, and shortly afterward another imperial city was added at nearby Persepolis (a city of which Herodotus seems unaware). To Persepolis, tribute flowed from all corners of the empire, according to a fixed schedule of sums levied yearly on each satrapy. Herodotus, who seems to have had access to an official copy of this schedule, records the levies in book 3, chapters 90–96, and though the numbers make dry reading, they give us a remarkable picture of the Persian state as tax assessor to the world—collecting the fabulous sum of 14,560 talents of silver each year (a single talent representing a handsome fortune to an average fifth-century Athenian). But a more eloquent testimony to the centralization of the empire is offered by the stone reliefs of the palaces at Persepolis, still standing amid the now-barren plains of this deserted Iranian site. In elegantly carved panels, ambassadors from the nations of the earth bring their

native products before the Great King: elaborate metallic ves-
sels from the Lydians, elephant tusks and exotic animals from
the Ethiopians, gold weighed out in panniers from the wealthy
Indians, and so on. Darius, whom the Persians ungenerously
referred to as a shopkeeper (perhaps "bureaucrat" would be
the best modern equivalent), succeeded, through his provincial
governors, in making Persepolis the treasury-house for the
world's riches and in administering a territory encompassing
no fewer than four of the largest empires that had preceded
him—Media, Babylon, Lydia, and Egypt. In the entire ancient
world, only the Romans would achieve a comparable feat of
imperial rule, and their system was in large part simply an
adaptation of that of Darius.

To further unite and centralize the empire, Darius undertook improvements in travel and communication. A canal leading eastward from the Nile into the Red Sea, first constructed
by the Egyptians but long since silted up, was now redug (see
Herodotus 2.158) and thereafter continued to allow sea passage between the Mediterranean and the Indian Ocean for another twelve hundred years (the present-day Suez Canal partly
follows its course). On land, an old highway connecting the
Persian capital Susa with Sardis, the largest imperial city in the
west, now became the Royal Road, a central corridor leading
through the heart of the empire. Along this thoroughfare a vast
system of station houses enabled royal messengers, traveling
in relays, to pass communiqués across the entire empire at
great speed. This system is described by Herodotus first in
book 5 (52–53) and again, in more detail, in book 8, and readers who arrive at this latter passage will be intrigued to discover that one aspect of Darius's empire has become a model
for today's U.S. government: the boast engraved above the
Federal Post Office building in New York, that "neither snow,
nor sleet, nor gloom of night stays the postman from his

appointed rounds," quotes Herodotus's description (8.98) of the Persian messengers who so faithfully carried the dispatches of the king.

In his foreign policy, Darius pursued a strategy of expansion as vigorously as his predecessor Cambyses had done. In the east he annexed parts of India as far as the Indus river. Herodotus tells fabulous tales about the Indians and their quest for gold (3.98–105) but says nothing about the military campaign that had led to this conquest. Instead, he focuses attention on Darius's bridging of the Bosporus and incursion into Europe, a project first mentioned at 3.134 and carried out in book 4. No one knows for certain what the goals of this expedition were or why Darius would have put so much expense and effort toward an attack on the nomadic Scythian tribes dwelling north of the Danube. Perhaps he meant only to establish a Persian beachhead in Europe by occupying Thrace, the land lying north of the straits of Bosporus, and crossed the Danube in a show of force to intimidate the Scythians; if so, then Herodotus has misrepresented a successful campaign as a near-catastrophic failure. In any case, the Scythians remained free, while the Thracians became the first European subjects of Persia. Darius then returned to Asia and left his general Megabazus to complete the conquest of Thrace and neighboring Paeonia, a campaign Herodotus describes at the beginning of book 5.

Megabazus also received the nominal submission of Macedonia, as Herodotus relates (5.17–22), but Persian authority in that semi-Hellenized kingdom was secretly undercut by the country's headstrong young prince, Alexander—the ancestor, as it happens, of another Alexander, who in 331 B.C. would defeat another Darius and bring the Achaemenid Persian empire to an end. Thus would Herodotus's dictum that great cities become small and small ones great be one day confirmed on a global scale. But for the mainland Greeks of the late sixth century, who now observed Darius's steady progress into the European lands just north of them, that day could not yet be imagined.

The growth and consolidation of the Persian empire, as related by Herodotus in the first half of the *Histories*, can be read either as a rags-to-riches success story or as a tale of reckless ambition and ill-conceived expansionism, or, more accurately, as both at the same time. Each of the three monarchs who had shaped the new state, Cyrus, Cambyses, and Darius, had vastly augmented its power, but each had died or met with disaster while venturing beyond its borders. The very rapidity of Cyrus's rise, moreover, had made enemies of those nations who either envied or feared him, such that unwilling subjects like Babylon and Egypt had to be subdued not once but multiple times. Finally, success abroad had led to factionalism at home: a conspiracy of Magian priests had briefly occupied the throne and had disrupted the peaceful transfer of dynastic power. All in all, by the midpoint of the *Histories*, the Persian empire has become a colossus that bestrides the world but stumbles and reels when it takes a step—whose very strengths, in other words, entail weaknesses and vulnerabilities, the historical irony that Herodotus will go on to explore in the second half of his work.

IV THE MAN AND
THE WORK

IN SPITE OF HERODOTUS'S MANY FIRST-PERSON COMMENTS IN the *Histories*—one scholar has reckoned them at more than a thousand—we know very little about the man himself or the circumstances of his life. "Did Herodotus have a *girlfriend?*" a student once asked me impatiently. We will never know the answer to this and many other questions. Herodotus seems to have been entirely lacking the impulse toward self-exploration that colors so much of modern literature and social discourse; he always directs his gaze outward, toward the world and its doings, never inward toward his own heart. The most subjective of the remarks he makes to his readers indicate only intellectual curiosity or surprise: "I am amazed," he says on numerous occasions in response to strange or unlikely stories, but otherwise he limits his comments to matters of judgment and factual record. And, in describing the cataclysmic events of 480 and 479 in his last three books, he indulges in no personal recollections, even though, if the date generally assumed for his birth is correct, he was as old as five or six at the time.

Perhaps the most important autobiographical information Herodotus gives his readers is contained in the opening two words of his text, "Herodotus of Halicarnassus." Here, in his "byline," Herodotus identifies himself as native to Halicarnassus, a Greek city on the southwest coast of Turkey that had been subject first to Lydian and then to Persian dominion. Yet not even this one vital datum comes down to us without complications, for in a different version of the opening sentence of the *Histories*, already known to and quoted by Aristotle in the fourth century, Herodotus identified himself as being "of Thurii," the Greek colony in southern Italy where he reportedly spent his later years. The two alternative openings represent two stages of Herodotus's life, his youth on the eastern perimeter of the Greek world and his maturity in the far west, and the fact that both were circulated in antiquity leaves us uncertain as to which place Herodotus more closely identified himself with. (Looked at in another context, this double tradition also supports the idea that Herodotus revised his work over the course of his life, an important issue I shall turn to shortly.)

As for what transpired between his birth in Halicarnassus and his migration to Thurii more than forty years later, we depend on the only partly reliable *Suda*, a Greek encyclopedia compiled in the Middle Ages from classical sources mostly now lost. The *Suda* tells us that Herodotus's family was prominent in Halicarnassus and included several people with non-Greek names, meaning that, like many in that region of Anatolia, he came from a mixture of Greek and native Carian lines. We are also told by the *Suda* that young Herodotus took part in an unsuccessful uprising against the local ruler, Lygdamis, and thereafter went into exile on the island of Samos, returning later in a second, successful coup against the tyrant. (The word "tyrant" here and elsewhere in this book should be understood as a translation of Greek *tyrannos*, "unconstitutional ruler," rather than in our more pejorative English sense of "despot.") If the story of Herodotus's struggle against Lygdamis is true, as seems likely given passages of the *Histories* that reveal a detailed knowledge of Samos, it would provide a context in which to read the many portraits in the *Histories* of overpowerful or arbitrary tyrants as well as the occasional hymns to the virtues of legally constituted regimes. Herodotus does, however, also paint an attractive portrait, in books 7 and 8, of Artemisia, the woman who had been puppet ruler in Halicarnassus under the Persians and who may have been the grandmother of Lygdamis. If Herodotus had in fact rebelled against this tyrant in his youth, he later shows remarkably little ill will toward his city's most famous tyrant—or indeed toward the whole idea of autocratic government (see chapter XII). So the *Suda*'s biographical information, even if it can be trusted, cannot easily be used to explain the content of the *Histories*.

At some point in his adult life Herodotus began to travel, though no one knows when or why or how he paid his way. It is possible he sailed on a merchant vessel and financed his voyages through trade; one scholar has called attention to Herodotus's keen eye for information about merchandise and shipping and speculated that he had a professional interest in such matters, though it might be objected that he had a keen eye for all human pursuits, trade included. In any case, it is clear from what he tells us himself that Herodotus had ready access to many distant lands and took full advantage of it. At different points in his book he claims to have made journeys to various parts of Egypt, to Olbia on the north shore of the Black Sea, and to Tyre on the Levantine coast; that he also visited Cyrene in North Africa and Babylon in Mesopotamia can probably be inferred from the detail of his descriptions. None of these far-flung lands, it should be said, would have been terribly difficult for a well-to-do fifth-century Hellene to visit; by the mid-400s, Greeks moved freely in the domain of their former enemy, Persia, and their drachmas could buy the assistance of native guides in Egypt and elsewhere. Herodotus's sheer breadth and virtuosity as a traveler are nonetheless astonishing. In one famous comment (2.44), he reports quite casually that his curiosity about the cult of Heracles led him to sail to Tyre, the site of a great temple dedicated to that god—as though there were nothing remarkable in making such a lengthy journey for the sake of researching a single point. His tone is similarly without vainglory when he reports having gone south through Egypt as far as Elephantine, near modern Aswan, in search of information about the upper course of the Nile (2.29). If we could be certain that he saw Babylon, we would have an even more striking instance of his offhandedness in matters of travel, for he says not a word about the weeks of arduous trekking he would have spent getting there. It would be as though Marco Polo, in medieval Italy, had given his account of China without saying anything about the journey there or back! It's possible, however, that Herodotus's description of Babylon in book 1 (178–86) was cribbed from some other source and then cleverly phrased in such a way as to imply that the author had been there himself. (Some scholars, though a small minority, accuse Herodotus of such cribbing even when he explicitly says he visited a place and have charged him, as now Marco Polo has also been charged, with inventing most or all of his travels.)

No more is known of Herodotus's wanderings until he ends up in Thurii, the city named in the alternate version of the *Histories'* opening sentence cited by Aristotle. This experimental Greek colony in the instep of the Italian boot was founded by Athens but included settlers from many Greek states, among whom were some of the leading intellectual figures of the day. Its establishment can be dated to 443, so Herodotus must have been past forty when he emigrated there; possibly he had already written the bulk of the *Histories* before that time, since in the work as we have it he makes only one brief reference to the lands and peoples of southern Italy (4.99). Thurii was said by some to contain Herodotus's grave, indicating perhaps that he remained there until his death, sometime after 430; but another city, Pella in Macedonia, also claimed his remains, so he may have left the golden west to return to the Greek mainland.

From about 485 to past 430: The span of Herodotus's life coincides almost precisely with the high classical age of the Greek world. Born just in time to witness the transformative Greek victory over Persia, Herodotus passed his adult life in a half century that saw rapidly increasing prosperity, an unprecedented efflorescence of the arts and of literature, and, thanks to the leadership of an increasingly powerful and egalitarian Athens, the spread of democracy to many formerly oligarchic Greek states. The growth of Athenian power during these fifty years, however, also created dangerous strains and oppositions that must have darkened the end of Herodotus's life. Relying on the same naval superiority that had enabled the Greek fleet to defeat the Persians, Athens began in the 470s to assert hegemony over the Aegean islands and Greek cities of Anatolia and Thrace. At first Athens maintained the pretense of leading these smaller states in a continuing defensive alliance against Persia, but after a time it became clear that they were really the subjects of a maritime empire, obliged to pay a yearly tribute just as they had under the Persian yoke. This new state of affairs made Athens a potential rival of the leading power in mainland Greece, Sparta, and the years from 465 on were marked by growing mistrust and conflict between the two former allies. Herodotus refers to the ominous trend when interpreting an earthquake that shook the sacred island of Delos during the first Persian invasion of Greece, in 490:

> This was the first and last earthquake Delos underwent up to my time. And this, I imagine, the god displayed as a portent to humankind of the ills that were to come: For in the reigns of Darius son of Hystaspes and Xerxes son of Darius and Artaxerxes son of Xerxes, in these three con-

secutive generations, more ills arose for Greece than in the
twenty generations preceding Darius; some arose there on
account of the Persians, and others from their own leading
cities, making war on each other over imperial power.
(6.98)

Herodotus here reveals, in a rare statement about his own times
(Artaxerxes reigned until 424), that the strife stirred up by the
Athens-Sparta rivalry was in some ways as grievous as that inflicted by the Persians in the previous generation. Eventually it
would lead to the so-called Peloponnesian War, a massive con-
flagration that ravaged all of Greece between 431 and 404 and
ended only after Athenian naval power was finally destroyed.

In what ways was Herodotus's historical perspective
shaped by this later war or by the rise of Athens to superpower
status through acquisition of an Aegean empire? He lived to
see at least the first few years of the Peloponnesian War and
perhaps as many as ten (the exact date of his death is a matter
of debate). Moreover, he had undoubtedly, at some point in his
life, spent time in the city of Athens (though the *Histories* gives
curiously little evidence of this) and may even have become
friends with the tragedian Sophocles and other leading Athenian artists and intellectuals. Above all, he could not have been
blind to the ways in which the imperialistic policies of Athens
during the mid–fifth century paralleled the behavior of Persia
several decades earlier; these parallels were evident to all in
the late 430s, to judge by Thucydides' record of the political
rhetoric of the day. Did Herodotus, then, write the story of Persia's downfall with Athens in mind or did he expect his audience, as the historian Kurt Raaflaub has recently claimed, "to
think of the present while they were hearing of the past"? Is the
whole of the *Histories* a long, veiled critique of Athenian empire building?

The answer to this last question, at least, must be no, although some would argue the point. It seems crucial to note that Herodotus, in avoiding explicit mention of events after 479 except in the few places where they bear directly on his story (e.g., 7.137, 8.3, 9.73), does not himself encourage the drawing of analogies between present and past or between Athens and Persia. Neither does his generally positive picture of Athenian naval leadership reveal much anxiety over the coming maritime empire (though there are ominous touches to his portrait of Themistocles, as we shall see in chapter XII). Hindsight has perhaps been the enemy of interpretation in this matter: we who know of the wholesale destruction of the Peloponnesian War from Thucydides' harrowing account are quick to see premonitions or preludes in everything that preceded it, but Herodotus might well have written most of the *Histories* before that war had seemed a certainty. What is more, his interest in recording the past, as expressed in his opening sentence, has far more to do with preserving the fame of that past than with providing paradigms for the future; though he is capable of deriving the most general lessons from history, such as his famous axiom "Human happiness never abides long in the same place" (1.5), he seems a long way off from the very particular moralizing or pattern-drawing of his Near Eastern contemporaries, the Hebrew prophets.

That said, however, it cannot be denied that the question of the fate of imperial Athens hovers spectrally over Herodotus's story of Persia, and very likely no fifth-century Greek could have ignored it. The trick for modern readers is to acknowledge this question's presence without allowing it to dominate their reading of the *Histories* or to resonate everywhere in the text. An analogy might be drawn to the interpretation of Shakespeare's historical dramas, many of which were played before Queen Elizabeth or King James and their courts.

Undoubtedly these plays raise questions about the correct use of royal power and thus contain implicit lessons for the monarchs who saw them performed. But to read them *only* as lessons, confined to a particular historical moment and circumstance, would be to ignore much of what has made them enduringly great. Such is the case also with Herodotus, a writer for whom contemporary politics formed but one of many frameworks for interpreting the past, and not at all the most important one.

The patchwork record of Herodotus's life has left us with many unanswered questions, though fortunately some of these do not diminish our ability to enjoy and understand the *Histories*. There is, however, one further biographical issue that anyone who reads his work with care will soon confront: How did Herodotus go about planning an enormously complex and difficult narrative task like the *Histories*, and how long did he spend composing it? That is, if we had his outlines or blueprints for the finished text, as we do, for example, for Joyce's *Ulysses*, what would they look like? How did he organize a work that was considerably longer and more wide-ranging than anything a Greek had written before? After all, he could follow only so far the structure supplied by the rise of Persia; he also had countless related but separate stories he wanted to tell and Greek history he needed to supply as background to the final showdown, and beyond these there was his *periodos gēs*, a tour of all the known world's lands and peoples— enough material for three or more separate works, if a less ambitious author had been drawing up the plans.

Indeed, there is some indication that Herodotus himself initially organized his material as several separate works. I have already referred to the theory that Herodotus wrote the Xerxiad, the tightly unified account of Xerxes' invasion that occupies books 7, 8, and 9, separately from and prior to the rest of the *Histories*. These books show greater coherence and continuity than the others, and on several occasions within them Herodotus introduces characters or terms as though unaware he had already dealt with them in previous books. It is easy to imagine, therefore, that he started out by writing an independent account of the events of 480 and 479—the most recent and therefore most easily researched of any he recorded—and only later, perhaps as a result of further travel, decided to incorporate that account into a much larger, more far-reaching work. A similar theory has been put forward concerning book 2 of the *Histories:* here, Herodotus freezes historical time at the moment the Persians are set to attack Egypt and conducts a long, detailed excursus on that land and its people; at the outset of book 3 he then restarts the clock as though merely continuing the narrative of book 1. It is again easy to imagine that Herodotus composed a separate work, *On Egypt,* after his travels there and later spliced it into the *Histories* where it best fit. Yet one might counterargue that the disjunctures between these two segments and the rest of the narrative are far less glaring than one would expect had they been written separately. Thus the question of whether the complete *Histories* reveals a unity with great internal diversity or a diversity with great unity is ultimately a judgment call, and different readers will see it in different ways.

However he put the pieces of the *Histories* together, it seems clear (although this point too has been disputed) that Herodotus went back over the whole to revise it and add bits of new information. Many short anecdotes or parentheses seem to have been wedged in between otherwise consecutive sentences, indicating that there were second or third "editions" of the text. (For this reason the references in books 7–9 to incidents in the Peloponnesian War, the very latest events Herodotus ever mentions, cannot be taken as proof that those books were written last.) During this revision process Herodotus may also have sought to bind his work together by adding cross-references from one segment to another. Thus, when recounting Egyptian religious practice in book 2, Herodotus describes the sacred bulls of Epaphus as being distinguished by certain characteristic markings "which I will relate in another section." Sure enough, the markings are later described in detail in book 3, when the Persian king Cambyses makes an attack on the Epaphus bull itself. If book 2 had originally been an independent work, Herodotus must have later added such links to make it cohere better with its new setting. His final revisions, though, seem to have been either careless or incomplete: in two famous cases he anticipates material that never actually appears in our text of the *Histories,* an account of the land and people of Assyria (mentioned twice, at 1.106 and 1.184) and the reason for the assassination of the traitor Ephialtes (7.213). These unfulfilled promises show either that Herodotus meant to keep adding to the *Histories* and was prevented or, alternatively, that he changed his mind about the scope of the work but then neglected to remove his initial cross-references.

From these scanty and sometimes ambiguous clues, then, one can infer that Herodotus worked on the *Histories* over much of his life and was still adding to it at the time of his death; and that he meant it to contain all his collected researches, including even material on Egypt that was initially framed as a separate study. As a man who saw the world whole, in other words, Herodotus knit his diverse interests together into an artistic unity, subsuming all within the grand pattern of the rise and decline of Persian power. Quite possibly he arrived at this unified scheme only in the middle of his career, however, and the task of melding his writings together and eliminating overlaps and conflicts cost him much effort.

Working on papyrus scrolls, a medium that makes editing and revising immensely difficult, he would have labored long and hard to get all his stories in the right sequence and to smooth over the seams and splices by which they were joined.

Further than this in the murky realm of biography and composition questions, it is neither safe nor desirable for this volume to go. Most such questions remain unresolved after more than a century of scholarly inquiry, and interested readers (especially those who know some Greek) can pursue them more closely in the works listed in the bibliography. For the present purposes, only these points are essential: The *Histories* we now have is in all major respects the work Herodotus meant us to have; he worked on it over a great length of time and substantially completed it. With that one stable platform on which to base our interpretations (and it is more than we have for many other ancient texts), we can give full attention in what follows to the work itself rather than to the author behind it; for that is certainly what Herodotus, the man who told us nothing else about himself than his name and homeland, intended us to do.

V THE DOWNFALL OF GREATNESS

Just as he tells us little about his own life in the *Histories*, so Herodotus rarely makes observations in his own voice about the patterns of history; usually he confines such philosophizing to the speeches he gives his characters. But in one crucial instance, right at the outset of his text, he allows himself a generalizing comment:

> After pointing out the man who *I* know was the first to begin unjust deeds against the Greeks, I shall move forward in my account, describing alike the small and large cities of humankind; for those that previously were large have for the most part become small, and those that were large in my time were small formerly. Understanding then that human happiness never abides in the same place, I shall mention both alike. (1.5)

Although he at first seems only to be explaining his editorial choices, Herodotus here discloses a vital piece of his thinking about the transitory nature of *eudaimoniē*, a word that means both "happiness" and "prosperity." Because the disappearance of *eudaimoniē* will be a central theme of his first story, the rise and fall of Croesus, his observation that it "never abides in the same place" reads like an epigraph for book 1 or possibly for the whole of the *Histories*. How, then, are we to understand this important comment?

59

"Good fortune doesn't last forever" may seem a tired or simplistic thought with which to preface a history of the world, the sort of sentiment that makes children sigh impatiently when they hear it repeated by parents; and yet there are good reasons, in Herodotus's time as in our own, for its repetition. Humankind tends toward a naive optimism that takes good things for granted and then expects even better to follow; unless we continually remind ourselves of the shifting nature of fortune, we will be caught off-guard by a downturn and utterly defeated. If our health is good we choose not to think about the times ahead when it will decline; if our finances thrive we spend more rather than save, ignoring the possibility of sudden reverses. So, even if Herodotus had no more to say about the lessons of history than not to expect good things to last, this message by itself might be worth hearing. But as we proceed into the text of the *Histories,* we shall find that beneath the seemingly banal statement lie deeper layers of thought.

For example, the word Herodotus introduces in the above passage, *eudaimoniē,* soon recurs in an even more prominent place: in a dialogue between Croesus and a Greek visitor to his court, the famous wise man Solon of Athens. Croesus, at the height of his power and wealth, takes Solon on a tour of his vast treasury and then asks him whom he considers the happiest of men; the Greek sage names not Croesus himself, but three comparative nobodies whose only distinction lay in having lived righteously and died in their prime. Herodotus then reports the following exchange:

Croesus became heated and said, "My Athenian guest, is our prosperity [*eudaimoniē*] thus discarded as worthless, that you put our value not even at that of private citizens?" And Solon said: "Croesus, when you asked me about the affairs of human life, you asked someone who knows that the divine is entirely jealous and likely to stir up trouble. In the long course of time, one will see many things and undergo many things one would not wish to."

There follows a long elaboration by Solon on the inevitable sorrows of human life and why wealth cannot make up for them, concluding with this advice:

One must look to the end of every matter, how it will turn out; for the god has shown a glimpse of happiness to many men, then destroyed them root and branch. (1.32)

In thus expressing the transitory nature of *eudaimoniē* Solon seems to echo the view Herodotus expresses in the preface to the *Histories* but adds greatly to its depth: in this larger formulation, the shifting of a person's fortunes is governed not by an impersonal or inevitable principle, but by the jealousy of the divine. "The god," by which name Solon denotes the sum total of deities known to the Greeks, here takes an active role in defeating human hopes and causing trouble where it is least expected. Consequently, the happiest men would be those whose lives Solon has just described: ordinary people who hoped for little and thus were not disappointed and who died before the god destroyed their happiness.

The fact that Solon's lecture on the evanescence of *eudaimoniē* comes so soon after Herodotus's own statement on the subject suggests that the created character here serves in part as spokesman for the author's own view; and this possibility becomes more likely as we read further and discover other wise men who seem to have been brought into the *Histories* only to expand on this idea. In book 3, for example, Amasis, an Egyptian pharaoh who had earlier been characterized by Herodotus as a somewhat shallow "good-time Charlie," suddenly

waxes philosophical in a letter he sends to Polycrates, the prosperous and powerful tyrant of Samos:

> Though in general it is sweet to hear that a friend and for-
> mer guest is doing well, your great good fortune does not
> please me, since I know that the divine is prone to jeal-
> ousy. Thus both for myself and for those I care about, I
> wish success in some enterprises and failure in others. . . .
> I've never heard tell of anyone who, after prospering in all
> things, did not in the end die miserably, root and branch.
> (3.40)

The Greek word translated "root and branch" here, *prorrizos*,
connects this letter with the above-quoted words of Solon to
Croesus, where the same unusual word and very similar ethical ideas first occur. Then in book 7, just as Xerxes is about to
launch his invasion of Greece, his uncle Artabanus restates the
same ideas (though this time in very different language) in an
attempt to dissuade him:

> You see how the god strikes oversized beasts with his
> thunderbolts and does not allow them their magnificence,
> while the small ones do not annoy him; you see how he al-
> ways throws his missiles at the tallest houses and at simi-
> larly vast trees. For the god tends to cut back anything
> oversized. And in the same way a great army is destroyed
> by a lesser, as follows: when the god grows jealous and
> casts panic into them or thunders, and thus they are dis-
> gracefully destroyed. For the god does not permit anyone
> but himself to think great thoughts. (7.10e)

These three meditations on divine jealousy, then, distrib-
uted through the text of the *Histories* as they are among the
peoples of the world—Solon, Amasis, and Artabanus, respec-
tively, represent the leading nations of Europe, Africa, and

Asia—form a set of variations on the theme first stated by Herodotus himself, that happiness never abides in the same place. What is more, in all three passages Herodotus himself almost certainly composed the words he gives to his characters: he could hardly have known, except perhaps in the vaguest terms, what had been said in councils of state and private letters half a century or more before his time. The conclusion seems inescapable, then, that Herodotus provided these three prominent commentaries on the downfall of greatness as a way of building an ethical framework around the events of the *Histories*, of giving a larger meaning to the events it records. (Of course, we cannot assume that Herodotus shares *all* sentiments expressed by his characters, any more than we can say Shakespeare concurs in all respects with Hamlet; but when a single idea recurs so prominently and often, in language that echoes the words first used by the author himself, we must certainly treat it as a keynote of the work.)

Indeed, the importance Herodotus gives to the words he assigns to Solon can be judged by the trouble he takes to include them, and Solon himself, in his narrative. The historical Solon did in fact travel abroad, as we know from other sources, but had returned to Athens and to private life well before the rise of Croesus in Lydia; he could never have had the conversation Herodotus depicts at the outset of book 1. But Solon's legendary reputation as a man of wisdom, piety, and moderation made him an ideal spokesman for the ethical themes of the *Histories*, and so Herodotus simply rearranges chronology in order to include him in the Croesus story—an artifice that was easily spotted by Plutarch, for one, and perhaps even by Herodotus's contemporaries. The whole scene between Solon and Croesus can in fact be seen as a forerunner of the philosophic dialogue later developed by Plato and Voltaire, in which famous historical personages are brought together, even in violation of chronology, in order to contrast their different points of view and highlight the one deemed superior. What is more, in order to ensure that his audience would not overlook the relevance of this dialogue, Herodotus later proclaims it a second time, in his account of Croesus's rescue from the funeral pyre. Here, in another episode that (as we have already seen) must have been embellished or even invented by Herodotus, Croesus is made to cry out, "Oh Solon!" in an agony of remorse, and then win redemption by repeating the Athenian's message to his captor, Cyrus—a message directed, as Croesus now realizes, as much toward all of humanity as toward himself (1.86). The entire story of Croesus's rise and fall, that is, has been constructed by Herodotus virtually as a case study of Solon's ethical ideas.

Once we begin to see the Croesus story in this way, we can better understand why Herodotus has, with considerable effort and determination, placed it first in his narrative sequence. To begin with Croesus, after all, meant stepping outside the time sequence and structure that govern the rest of his text, starting from the birth of Cyrus; it would have been easier and more natural to start book 1 with Cyrus and then give an account of Croesus at the point in Cyrus's life where the Persians conquer Lydia (much as the land of Egypt is introduced at the moment when Cyrus's son, Cambyses, invades it). Instead, Herodotus levers the Croesus story out of its place in Persian history and moves it to the opening position, as if making it an overture to the grand opera that follows. Indeed, like an overture, this section establishes the tone and highlights the motifs that will be central to the rest of the work. It follows the career of one person who rose to greatness, who failed to understand the jealous nature of divinity, and who was utterly defeated and cast down; thus it establishes a paradigm in miniature for

the rise and decline of the Persian empire, the subject of the re-
mainder of the *Histories*.

But Herodotus supplies more than one explanation for
Croesus's downfall; Solon's principle of divine jealousy, what
the Greeks called *phthonos*, is not the only force at work. As Herodotus tells us at the outset of the story, Croesus's great-great-
grandfather Gyges had come to power by murdering the
rightful Lydian ruler, Candaules. An oracle thereafter reported
to Gyges but soon forgotten by him predicted that his descendants would pay a retribution, or *tisis*, in the fifth generation
(1.13). Thus, although Croesus's life was ultimately spared in
the miraculous rescue from the pyre, Herodotus leaves us in no
doubt that his downfall *had* to happen in order for that old
score to be settled. And just as he does in the case of Solon's
message, Herodotus underscores this point by repeating it: in
the final episode of the Croesus story we hear the Delphic oracle explain that "Croesus paid for the crime of his ancestor in
the fifth generation, who . . . killed his master and took the royal
power though it was not rightfully his" (1.91). This principle of
tisis, or payback, must be distinguished from what Solon has
said about divine jealousy, *phthonos*, in that *tisis* has stronger
ethical force: it is because Gyges seized power *wrongly*, not
simply because he became overpowerful, that his descendant
Croesus was brought low. However, Herodotus also allows the
two ideas to overlap or blend because he conceives of greatness or unrestrained power as itself a kind of moral transgres-
sion. That is to say, Herodotus believes that the Solonic balance
in the world of human affairs has both divine and moral sanc-
tion; to disrupt it, as Croesus did when he sought to dominate
Asia, is to invite the wrath of a spiteful deity *and* the retribution
of injured justice. Greatness, by its very nature, violates this
balance and calls down upon itself a retribution that reduces it

to smallness, as in the case of the towering tree and ramping lion described by Artabanus.

But is it fair to assume that animals and even plants are governed by the same moral laws as humankind? In Herodotus's worldview, the answer must be yes; for in his eyes, these creatures fall from greatness in the same ways that human beings do, as illustrated in the following discussion of the different reproductive rates of different species:

> It seems that the forethought of the divine, being (as is reasonable) wise, has made prolific all the creatures that are timid in spirit and that serve as prey, so that they may not be devoured and die out; but it has made unprolific those that are savage and dangerous. On the one hand the hare, being prey to every kind of beast and to bird and man, is prolific to this extent: It alone of all beasts can conceive while already pregnant. . . . On the other hand the lioness, being boldest and most violent, bears one cub once in its life; for when it gives birth it expels its womb along with its young. And the cause of this is as follows: When the cub begins stirring inside its mother, since it has the sharpest claws by far of any creature, it scratches her womb, and as it grows it pierces all the more when it scratches; by the time of birth there is nothing left sound of her womb at all. It's the same with vipers and the winged snakes in Arabia. . . . When they are yoked in copulation and the male, in the very act of procreation, discharges his seed, the female seizes his neck and clings tightly, not letting go until she gnaws right through. The male dies in the manner thus described, but the female pays back a retribution [*tisis*] to the male: For the children avenge their sire while still inside their mother, eating through her womb and destroying her belly as they make their exit. (3.108)

Ignoring for now Herodotus's mistaken notions about the animal world, let us note how both these accounts of natural history follow the same ethical patterns that the wise men of the *Histories* perceive in national history. The lion gains its supreme power in part from the sharpness of its claws, yet this very strength carries with it a counterbalancing limitation; the hare, by contrast, flourishes in proportion to its defenselessness. This paradigm elegantly translates into biological terms the workings of Artabanus's jealous divinity, the god who hurls thunderbolts at the great and mighty beasts but is not chafed by meek ones. Meanwhile, the viper, like the lion, has its population kept in balance by the high costs of its reproductive process, but in this case the balance is more highly fraught with moral significance, as indicated by Herodotus's use of the term *tisis*. The natural ferocity of the species leads the female to destroy the male as he impregnates her; but a brood of young avengers then settles the score as they bore their way out of her womb. Both lion and viper are said to be governed by a wise "forethought of divinity," but that power acts in very different ways in the two cases, corresponding to the *phthonos* and *tisis* that combine to destroy Croesus.

These related ideas of divine balance and moral retribution pervade Herodotus's understanding of the cosmos, and so they appear everywhere within the text of the *Histories;* though seemingly simple, they recur, like a triadic chord in a Mozart opera, in endless and untiring diversity. Once readers have accustomed their ears to this chord they will begin to hear its rich harmonies everywhere, not only in the text of Herodotus but in the world around them as well. Though we moderns are unused to the idea of a divinity that can experience jealousy and thus may at first feel estranged from the god of Artabanus who blasts great beings with his thunderbolts, we can easily appreciate the more abstract ways in which the same balancing principle gets expressed. In the realm of biological science, for example, our own recent experience closely parallels Herodotus's notion of a divine forethought that keeps predators in check: for the growth of human populations in the past century is now seen to threaten the survival of less powerful creatures and at the same time to invite a kind of counterdestruction in the form of viral outbreaks, resource shortages, and other environmental disasters. Indeed, among some biologists the seeming hostility of our planet toward species, like *Homo sapiens*, that outgrow their niches has been dubbed Gaia after the ancient Greek goddess of the earth—demonstrating that an impersonal balancing mechanism can, even today, be personified as a powerful or vengeful divinity.

But the downfall of greatness, as portrayed by Herodotus, presents something more than the satisfying but hardly compelling spectacle of evil deeds being punished or of cosmic equilibrium being restored. The eastern rulers who meet disaster or defeat in the *Histories* must also be seen as tragic heroes, similar in some important respects to the rulers portrayed in Athenian dramas (Xerxes, in fact, is a tragic hero in the literal sense, his defeat having been staged as drama by Aeschylus in *The Persians*). Herodotus allows us to feel pity and fear for these figures, the emotions identified by Aristotle as central to the tragic experience, by showing us the web of circumstance that has inexorably wrought their ruin; though each is partly responsible for his own fate, each is also a victim of forces beyond his control. Let us take the paradigmatic Croesus once again as an example. After his conversation with Solon, during which he fails to heed any of the wisdom he is offered, Croesus is visited by what Herodotus calls "a vengeance from god, because, as it seems, he thought himself to be the happiest of all men" (1.34). A stranger named Adrastus appears at Croesus's court seeking to be cleansed of the stain of fratricide;

Croesus graciously takes him in and performs the rites that will allow Adrastus to live in society once again despite his crime. The stranger's name sounds an ominous note, however, because Adrastus can mean "he who cannot be escaped," and the feminine form of the same name is elsewhere used as an epithet of Nemesis, the personification of divine vengeance. Sure enough, before long Adrastus unwittingly causes the death of Croesus's beloved son Atys, an event Croesus had foreseen in a dream and had taken great pains to prevent. In a final scene that reads very much like the plot summary of a tragic drama, Croesus mourns over the body of his fallen son and pardons Adrastus, saying, "It is not you who are the cause of this misfortune, but one of the gods, who long ago fore-warned me what was to be"; Adrastus nevertheless slays him-self over the tomb of his unintended victim. All three men have become caught up in a nexus of divine forces so malign that even a noble deed like Croesus's purification of Adrastus leads to the direst of consequences. The gods who elsewhere preside over cosmic balance here appear not to have evened the score, but to have punished many times over Croesus's presumption in thinking himself most fortunate.

The case of Polycrates, tyrant of Samos, offers another and in some ways more disturbing example of a man caught in the tragic web. Polycrates, like Croesus, is warned by a wise moralist—the Egyptian pharaoh Amasis—about the jealous ways of divinity, but, unlike Croesus, he elects to heed the warnings. On Amasis's suggestion, Polycrates takes his most precious possession, a gold ring set with an emerald, and casts it into the sea. Some days later a fisherman appears at the palace door and presents him with a newly caught fish—and in its belly is found the same gold ring! On hearing of this miraculous recovery, the pharaoh Amasis concludes "that no man could rescue another from what was going to happen to him, and that Polycrates was coming to a bad end"; the hapless Polycrates is soon thereafter entrapped and executed by his Persian neighbors. Amasis's depiction of this downfall as "what was going to happen" recalls the language Croesus uses to describe the inevitability of the loss of his son, but Polycrates seems to deserve his sufferings even less than Croesus did; he had, after all, sought to appease the jealous gods by willingly mitigating his good fortune. The iron laws of *tisis* and *phthonos* become despotic when they punish even those who try earnestly to obey them.

Herodotus was a close contemporary and perhaps even a friend of Sophocles, as we have seen, so it is no wonder he adapted patterns from tragic drama for use in his newly invented literary medium. If he has drawn on the heroes of tragedy in portraying ill-fated kings like Croesus, moreover, he has similarly taken the tragic chorus as a model for the wise advisors who point out the errors of their ways. The chorus of a tragedy, representing average people very much like the spectators in a Greek audience, typically express pity and horror at the action unfolding on stage, yet at the same time remain detached from it: "Not for me the perils of wealth and power; let me live a modest and quiet life," they say in various ways in many extant dramas. The similarities between these sentiments and the speech of Solon to Croesus in the *Histories*, with its praise of ordinary men who had lived and died in relative obscurity, are unmistakable. Later, Croesus himself, having learned the value of Solon's wisdom, becomes a kind of chorus leader as he accompanies the Persian rulers Cyrus and Cambyses on their campaigns. In a long speech at the end of book 1, for example, Croesus claims that "my sufferings, though bitter, have become my lessons" and tries to impart his hard-won wisdom to Cyrus:

If you think yourself to be immortal and the leader of an immortal army, there would be no point in my revealing my opinion to you; but if you recognize that you, too, are human and you command others like yourself, then above all heed this: There is a wheel of human affairs, and as it spins round it does not always allow the same men to succeed. (1.207)

Croesus has here become wise enough to echo the idea of fortune's mutability, first expressed by Herodotus himself in the preface to the *Histories*; in other words, he has been transformed into one of the sages who stand at the periphery of historical action, breaking in here and there with moral commentary, just as a tragic chorus breaks into the action of a drama. Indeed, Croesus's words strike very much the same note as a beautiful choral ode in a tragedy by Sophocles, a play Herodotus might well have seen or read:

Nothing painless
has the all-ruling king, Zeus son of Kronos,
imposed on mortal men;
Rather, grief and joy come circling to all,
like the wheeling track
of the Great Bear's stars.

Glittering night does not remain
for mortals, nor does doom nor wealth;
All at once they are gone, and it comes to another
to feel joy and its loss. (*Women of Trachis* lines 126–36)

Croesus further exemplifies the viewpoint of the tragic chorus in that he alone, of all the doomed kings in the *Histories*, claims to have learned from his downfall. The words in which Croesus expresses this transformation ("my *pathēmata* [sufferings] have become *mathēmata* [lessons]," he says in a kind of jingle) closely echo a famous line from a choral ode of Aeschylus's *Agamemnon*, in which the gods' plan for humankind is defined as "learning through suffering" (*pathei mathos*). Unfortunately, he seems unable to translate that learning into sound practice, for the advice he goes on to give his master Cyrus leads to the destruction of an entire Persian army and to Cyrus's own gruesome death. But what is important here is that Herodotus bestows on Croesus a kind of insight into the ways of fortune, a wisdom born of having watched his own empire rise and fall—the same wisdom, significantly enough, that Herodotus himself proclaims at the opening of the *Histories*.

Much as I have tried here to isolate the idea of a tragic fate that governs the downfall of Herodotus's monarchs and tyrants, this notion cannot always be clearly distinguished from that of *tisis*, or retribution, for wrongdoing—any more than *tisis* can itself be neatly separated from the idea of divine jealousy. The death of Cambyses in book 3, for example, shows how easily fate and retribution shade into one another. Cambyses, en route to Persia to quell a rebellion there, inflicts a mortal wound on himself while mounting his horse; he then learns that the town he has arrived at is Ecbatana, not the famous Median capital but a Syrian city of the same name. He recalls an oracle that had long ago predicted his death would come in Ecbatana and, realizing that he had wrongly assumed the Median town was meant, grimly announces, "Here is the place that Cambyses, son of Cyrus, is fated to die." What he seems not to have realized, however, is the significance of his wound, as pointed out to us by Herodotus: he has stabbed himself in the exact same spot that he had earlier stabbed the Apis, a calf sacred to the Egyptians. At one and the same moment, that is, Cambyses fulfills the destiny predicted for him long before and repays with his own life the life he had so impiously taken. He dies with the same words on his lips that Croesus utters in mourning the loss of his son and that Amasis pronounces in response to Polycrates' good fortune: "I see now that it was not within the power of human nature to turn aside that which was going to be" (3.65)—failing, once again, to recognize that his own atrocities had put him in harm's way.

At times, Herodotus flirts with the idea of an impersonal fate utterly indifferent to the moral qualities of those whom it governs, and this is perhaps the most disturbing of all the ways in which he accounts for the downfall of greatness. If this idea were more prevalent in the *Histories*, we might be justified in speaking of Herodotus's nihilism, but it is limited to isolated moments and minor characters. Consider, however, the dark world where dwells the Egyptian pharaoh Mycerinus, whose story is told in a few brief chapters of book 2. Herodotus portrays Mycerinus as a saint among rulers: he freed peoples enslaved by the two despotic pharaohs who preceded him (his father and uncle) and restored temples that had been shut by these men for more than a century; he judged lawsuits virtuously and sometimes even made good the losses of litigants out of his own pocket. Nevertheless, like Croesus he was forced to undergo the cruelest of human sufferings, the loss of a beloved child. And worse was yet to come:

> An oracle came to him from the city of Buto, saying that he would live six more years and die in the seventh. Mycerinus took this ill and sent to the oracle a rebuke to the god, reproaching him in reply that his own father and uncle had sealed off the temples and disregarded the gods, and had harmed their people, yet had lived a long life; whereas he himself had been pious, yet was about to die in so short a time. A second message then came from

the oracle, telling him that it was for that very reason that his life was hastening to a close: He had not done what it was fated for him to do; for it was necessary that Egypt suffer for 150 years, and the two kings preceding him had known that, whereas he had not. (2.133)

Mycerinus, again like Croesus, receives a divine theodicy that explains the meaning of his downfall, but the explanation is such as to lead him not to wisdom but to an impotent form of rebellion: he lives out his remaining time staying up all night and never ceasing from food, drink, and pleasure, thus giving the lie to the oracle by seeming to live twelve years instead of six. Here, then, is a story taken not from the tragic world of Sophocles but from the existential comedy of a Sartre or a Beckett, depicting a helpless individual's struggle to keep his dignity in a senseless universe.

Readers of the *Histories* often feel troubled by the diversity of these sometimes overlapping, sometimes conflicting explanations of the ruin of kings, but we should not expect any coherent or consistent scheme to emerge from them. Herodotus was an observer of life, not a moral philosopher, and his observations revealed to him a multiplicity of reasons for the downfall of greatness. The roots of personal disaster are, after all, terribly difficult to uncover, as those who have endured them or who have helped others to do so can attest. Parents who undergo the loss of a child, for example, may at one moment see themselves in the position of Croesus, paying a terrible price for taking happiness too much for granted; at the next moment Mycerinus, the victim of a blind, amoral destiny, may seem a more accurate paradigm. Is the fault behind such disasters in our stars or in ourselves? Are we being punished for some wrongdoing or has the wheel of fortune merely taken an unlucky turn, someday to turn back in the opposite direction?

Few misfortunes can be easily rationalized in one way or another, and we oversimplify them at our peril; even if we had a Delphic oracle, as Croesus had, to anatomize our losses, its message might not be easy to understand. In the end the only truth that can be distilled from this welter of possibilities is the one stated by Herodotus at the outset of his text: No human happiness endures forever.

Nor unhappiness either, he might have said. But Herodotus pays little attention to people whose fortunes change for the better or those who, like the Egyptian pharaoh Amasis, have the good luck to live long and yet avoid troubles (3.10). Even Croesus, if measured according to the Solonic precept "Look to the end in all things," might have been accounted a happy man: he ends his life, as far as Herodotus knows, an honored and trusted advisor to the Persian crown, and his legendary wealth may well have been passed on to his heirs (if, as some scholars assume, the rich Lydians Atys and Pythius mentioned at 7.27 and following are Croesus's descendants). But the *Histories* gives us no account of Croesus's presumably peaceful death that might allow us to make a new and more positive assessment of his life. What remains central for Herodotus is the downward stroke of the cosmic leveling mechanism, even though, by his own formulation, every such downswing implies an upswing elsewhere. Similarly, at the national level, he chose to recount the conflict between Greece and Persia more as a tale of Persian defeat than of Greek victory, just as Aeschylus had done in his tragedy *The Persians,* and to make the Persian kings, each of whom came to a bad end or saw his greatest undertakings end in defeat, the main characters of that story.

It has been said that Herodotus exhibits the sunnier, more cheerful side of the Hellenic temperament, in contrast to the brooding pessimism of Thucydides, and this is true to a certain degree. Readers of the *Histories* are not forced to confront the nightmarish agonies that Thucydides chronicles in brutal detail and are offered the considerable comfort that a wise divinity governs the world. We should bear in mind, however, that even the sunniest Greek temperament pales when set against the radiant optimism that suffuses much of modern American life. Solon's somber lesson to Croesus, that much of human happiness is either created or, more likely, destroyed by events beyond human control, is hard for us to hear in an age of self-reliance and self-improvement, yet Herodotus would tell us that we ignore it at our peril. He often says of one of his characters, "Things were destined to go badly for him," implying that an individual's activities or ambitions inevitably caused him to run afoul of this element of chance. By contrast, he never says of anyone in the *Histories*—one cannot imagine him saying—"Things were destined to turn out well."

VI THE STRUCTURE OF THE EARTH

AMONG THE MANY NOTES SOUNDED IN SOLON'S GREAT MEDITA-tion on the nature of happiness, one important idea has thus far gone unmentioned. Toward the end of his last speech to Croesus, as he is reaching his rhetorical climax, Solon formulates his main theme, the balance of good and bad that defines human life, in a striking new way:

> It's not possible for any human being to have all good things at once, just as no land is so self-sufficient as to produce everything it needs; each land has different resources, but all lack something; whichever one has the most, that one is the best. Just so no one human body is self-sufficient; it has one thing but lacks another. (1.32)

This example from the realm of geography, in which lands of the earth become analogues for individual human beings, is the first of many interconnections between micro- and macrocosm that Herodotus will explore in the *Histories*. The earth itself, what Herodotus calls the *oikeomenē*, or "inhabited world," will be one of his main concerns, not merely because he intends to supply interesting new information about it, but because in his eyes its very structure and makeup participate in the same moral scheme that defines human life. Just as he does with the creatures of the natural world, that is—the lions and vipers whose reproductive patterns parallel the rise and fall of tyrants—so with lands, seas, mountains, rivers, winds, and tides

Herodotus constructs a system that reflects "the forethought of the divine" and provides an ethical framework for history.

Herodotus, in fact, restates in his own voice Solon's point about the balance of the earth's resources, in the same passage of book 3 that describes lion and snake reproduction. Here, in introducing a long digression on the riches harvested in distant lands, Herodotus observes that

> the furthest parts of the *oikeomenē*, it seems, have as their portion the finest things, just as Greece has very much the best mixture of seasons. (3.106)

The great balancing principle we looked at in the last chapter is here applied by Herodotus on a grand scale, such that it defines the very structure of the earth: lands lying at the center, including Greece itself, enjoy a moderate climate but are poor in natural resources, while those at the perimeter experience the opposite. India, for example—a land Herodotus knew only from vague reports at second or third hand—has harsh extremes of temperature, scorchingly hot in the daytime and cold at night; but its people prosper by collecting gold, stealing it from the ferocious "ants" that heap up great ore-rich mounds outside their burrows (3.103–5). (The curious tale of the Indian ants, said to be smaller than dogs but larger than foxes, has been borne out recently by the discovery that a species of marmot in the highlands of Pakistan does, in fact, leave mounds of gold-rich earth outside its burrows; it is even possible that this very creature was known as "mountain-ant" to the ancient Persians.) Likewise in the far North, cold and damp weather is counterbalanced by an abundance of gold, said to be harvested in a similar manner. According to legends Herodotus repeats only mistrustfully, one-eyed Arimaspians steal this gold from the lairs of dragonlike creatures called griffins (3.116). "Thus," Herodotus concludes, closing off the discussion with a sentence that matches its opening, "the furthest lands, which enclose the rest of the earth and shut it inside, have the things that we judge the best and most rare." Though he does not attribute this balance between center and rim to any particular agent, it seems clear that the same "forethought of the divine" that governs snake and lion births, as explained in a passage that falls midway between these two "bookend" sentences, helps determine larger world structure.

Not only is the distribution of the earth's resources governed by divine forethought, moreover, but also its very configuration, the arrangement of land and water that determines its continents, islands, and peninsulas. In an episode near the beginning of the *Histories* (1.174), Herodotus illustrates the perils of attempting to alter this divinely sanctioned topography. While the Persians are preparing to attack the Greek cities of the Anatolian coast, one such city, Cnidos, attempts to cut itself off from the mainland by digging a canal across a thin isthmus. The workmen chiseling away at the rocky isthmus keep getting injured by flying splinters, and the accident rate climbs so high that the city sends to Delphi for advice. The oracle tells them they must stop digging, for "Zeus would have made an island, if he had wanted." One is reminded of the horror with which Shakespeare's Welsh sorcerer Glendower greets the suggestion of Hotspur, that the course of the river Trent be altered to even out two parcels of land:

> *Hotspur*. It shall not wind with such a deep indent
> To rob me of so rich a bottom, here.
> *Glendower*. Not wind? It shall, it *must!* You see it doth.

That "it doth" resonates with the same outrage expressed by Apollo's oracle in Herodotus: The topography of the world has been established by divinity and man insults that divinity by tampering with it; our capacity to reshape the earth is a form of *hybris* that sets us at odds with the natural order of things. And lest we doubt that the view of the oracle is shared by Herodotus himself, the historian later makes a similar observation in his own voice: when King Xerxes cuts a canal through the peninsula of Athos, says Herodotus, "he ordered it to be dug on account of his pridefulness, wishing to display his power and leave a memorial behind; for the Persians could have dragged their ships across the isthmus without taking any trouble at all" (7.24). Though he charges Xerxes only with "pridefulness" here, using a much weaker and more ambivalent term than *hybris*, his tone clearly registers disapproval of this alteration of the structure of the earth.

If it is presumptuous to cut off an isthmus by a canal, according to Herodotus, the structural inverse of this act, the bridging of a strait or river, can be equally presumptuous. Such bodies of water form the natural boundaries between peoples and territories, so that to render crossable those that formerly could not be crossed seriously upsets the earth's natural order. Herodotus thus portrays nearly all his expansionist kings and tyrants as reckless water-crossers and lingers in fascination over the moments when they must, so to speak, cross the Rubicon. Let us look, for example, at how the motif of river crossings defines the career of Cyrus in book 1. First, while moving on Babylon, Cyrus is attempting to cross the river Gyndes when one of his sacred white horses, acting out of what Herodotus calls *hybris*, attempts to ford the stream and is washed away by it. Cyrus feels that the river has now committed an act of *hybris* against *him* and vows revenge: threatening to make the Gyndes "so weak that from now on even women can cross it easily, without wetting their knees" (1.189), Cyrus orders his army to divide the water into 360 channels, a task that takes them all summer to complete. This is just the sort of megalomania that ordinarily costs a Herodotean ruler dear, but Cyrus goes on to mount a successful campaign against Babylon—indeed, he takes the city by a stratagem that echoes his punishment of the Gyndes, diverting the river Euphrates from its customary course and then advancing along the riverbed and under the city walls (1.191).

In his next campaign, though, against the Massagetae on his northeastern borders, Cyrus finally crosses a river too far. The Araxes river forms the Persian boundary with the Massagetae and also, in Herodotus's view, the boundary between Europe and Asia: like other Greek geographers, Herodotus thought of Europe as stretching across the whole northern portion of the *oikeomenē*, limited not by the Ural Mountains to the east but by the Caspian Sea and other bodies of water to the south. Understandably, then, Cyrus hesitates before crossing the Araxes, and his counselors advise him to stand his ground and allow his enemies to cross over instead, as they have offered to do. But here Herodotus reports that Croesus, who has by this time become a friend and advisor to the Persian crown, intervenes to change Cyrus's mind (an episode discussed in the previous chapter). The Persians forge ahead across the Araxes and are destroyed on the other side, and Cyrus himself is slain, his corpse left to be cruelly defiled by the Massagetan queen. Although Herodotus does not explicitly link Cyrus's downfall to his crossing of the Araxes, the debate that precedes that crossing underscores its momentousness: by traversing the boundary between Europe and Asia, Cyrus transgresses a moral law embedded in the very structure of the earth.

The pattern illustrated by the death of Cyrus, in which an arrogant river crossing leads to destruction and defeat, takes on much larger dimensions from book 4 onward, when first Darius and then Xerxes undertake similar projects on a much grander scale: the bridging of the Hellespont (now known as the Dardanelles) and the Bosporus to form invasion routes into

Europe. Though today we may think little of the fact that Turkey spills across these two straits and straddles the continents, Herodotus portrays the divide between Asian Anatolia and European Thrace as a natural and divinely sanctioned state of affairs. Indeed, the entire story of the *Histories* from book 4 on can be described as Persia's unsuccessful challenge to the separation of the continents, its attempt to make political geography supersede what is natural. First in Darius's attack on the Scythians, then in his seaborne assault on the Greek mainland, and finally in Xerxes' much larger invasion of Greece by land and sea, we see the Persians struggling to overcome the natural limits that they themselves had originally accepted, according to information Herodotus gives at the very outset of the *Histories:*

> The Persians claim as their own Asia and the barbarian tribes living within it, and regard Europe and Greek territory as something separate from this. (1.4)

Asia belonged to the Persians, in their minds at least, by a kind of manifest destiny—and we must understand "Asia" here to include Egypt and North Africa because in Herodotus's scheme, as expressed (though in very confusing language) at 2.17 and 4.41, these territories are really peninsular extensions of Asia rather than parts of a separate African continent. (At 4.45 Herodotus agrees to use the customary division of three continents so as to accommodate his audience and hence refers to Libya, or Africa, throughout as though it were separate from Asia, but clearly he doesn't accept this separation himself.) Had the Persians obeyed this destiny, Herodotus seems to imply, they might never have come to grief; but in their restlessness to expand they transgressed continental limits, both in the East, with Cyrus's fording of the Araxes, and in the West, with Darius's and Xerxes' crossings of the straits.

The first of these two crossings, Darius's bridging of the Bosporus, is described only sketchily by Herodotus (4.87–89), but the general approach is clear enough: a Greek engineer, Mandrocles of Samos, is employed to fasten a line of ships together such that an army could march across on their decks. His method was probably similar to that later used by Xerxes' engineers to bridge the Hellespont, as described in detail by Herodotus in book 7:

> They set together penteconters and triremes [two types of warship], 360 for the bridge nearer the Black Sea and 314 for the other. . . . After that they let down long anchors. . . . They left a navigable opening through the penteconters, so that those who wished might sail into or out of the Black Sea in small craft. Having done this they stretched ropes from the land and tightened them with wooden winches. . . . When the strait was thus bridged, they cut up wooden logs and made them equal in width to the pontoon-bridge and set them atop the cables, then, having set them there in a row, they fastened them down a second time [i.e., with cross-beams?]. Next they put brushwood on top, smoothed it out and put earth on top of the brushwood and packed the earth down; and they laid a fence along either side so that the pack animals would not panic, seeing the sea below them. (7.36)

The ancient world had never before seen such an ambitious bridge as the one built by Mandrocles, and Darius, according to Herodotus, celebrated its construction by heaping riches on the engineer; Mandrocles took this reward money and commissioned a painting of the bridge that he dedicated in his native Samos as a memorial to the goddess Hera. Doubtless he wished to publicize his achievement before his fellow citizens, but the piety of the gesture is also noteworthy: at the moment of his greatest glory, the reverent Mandrocles subordinates himself to the gods, thereby avoiding the taint of *hybris*.

How different is the attitude of Xerxes when throwing *his* bridges across the Hellespont! Xerxes seems to regard passage across this strait as his prerogative and becomes enraged when a storm washes away his initial efforts. This violent storm, like the flying rock splinters of the Cnidos canal, seems to represent the displeasure of divinity at seeing the earth reshaped, as if nature itself were rejecting Xerxes' bridge the way a human body rejects a transplant. But the impetuous king scorns the will of the divine and insists on having his way. As Herodotus reports, Xerxes orders his men to flog the water of the Hellespont and throw fetters into it, perhaps even to brand it with hot irons, and to insult it by saying: "You bitter water! Your master punishes you thus because you wronged him, though you received no wrong from him. Yet King Xerxes will cross you, whether you will it or no. It's fitting, we now see, that no one sacrifices to you, since you are both a muddy and a salty river" (7.35). In the end, Xerxes completes his bridge, using stronger cables against the power of the storm. But the offense he has committed in punishing the Hellespont leaves an indelible taint. After the great naval bridge has been completed and the Persians prepare to cross, Herodotus describes a portent that seems to seal the doom of Xerxes and his expedition: "The sun left its place in the sky and disappeared, though there were no clouds and the air was especially clear, and it became night instead of day" (7.37). The language here suggests not a solar eclipse (elsewhere in the *Histories* a readily intelligible phenomenon), but a *disappearance* of the sun, as if nature itself had turned its face away from the act Xerxes was about to commit.

Beyond these signs and omens, Herodotus goes further in showing us that Xerxes' behavior at the Hellespont embodies

the larger *hybris* of Persian imperialism—just as Aeschylus in
the *Oresteia* shows through Agamemnon's famous decision to
tread on a purple robe the haughty spirit that led to the attack
on Troy. Herodotus describes the insults hurled by Xerxes' men
at the river as "reckless and barbarian words," the only occasion in the *Histories* in which he openly reproaches the Persians
for not behaving like Greeks. (In the *Oresteia*'s robe-treading
scene just mentioned, Aeschylus has Agamemnon refer to his
impious action as "the mark of a barbarian" before hesitantly
agreeing to perform it.) With this anomalously pejorative use
of the word *barbaros,* Herodotus conjures up all the arrogance,
presumption, and expansionist greed associated by the Greeks
with the Asiatic temperament. And the barbed epithet sticks to
its target, even though Herodotus later concedes the possibility that Xerxes regretted his action and made amends to the
Hellespont (7.54). In fact, Herodotus's condemnation of Xerxes'
behavior is later echoed in a speech delivered by a Greek commander, Themistocles the Athenian, in book 8. After master-
minding the Greek victory at Salamis, Themistocles recalls
Xerxes' behavior at the Hellespont as a way of explaining the
miraculous outcome of the battle:

> *We* have not accomplished these things, but the gods and
> heroes, who begrudge that a single man should rule both
> Europe and Asia, and what's more an impious and reck-
> less man: for he has been treating the divine shrines as
> though they were private property, burning them and
> overturning the statues of the gods; and he flogged the sea
> and threw fetters into it. (8.109)

Unfortunately, Themistocles cannot be taken entirely at his
word in this important speech because Herodotus reveals that
it has a hidden purpose: to dissuade the Greeks from pursuing
the Persian navy and thus allow Themistocles to put Xerxes in

his debt. But whatever the speaker's motive, the words have been chosen in an effort to convince, and we have no reason to doubt the validity of the main idea they express: that a divine order keeps Europe and Asia under separate political control and looks upon the forcing of the boundary between those realms as an act of sacrilege.

Both Darius in book 4 and Xerxes in books 7–9 come to grief in Europe, and their elaborately built thoroughfares over the Bosporus and Hellespont become tenuous lifelines for their retreating armies. In both cases, the Greeks contemplate the strategy of breaking down the bridges and cutting off the Persian escape route; in fact, the fate of Darius's entire army comes to rest on the goodwill of a single individual, Histiaeus of Miletus, as the royal advisor Artabanus later points out (7.10). And though Darius succeeds in establishing a Persian beachhead in Europe that endures for several decades, the severing of the continents becomes final and permanent following the defeat of Xerxes' armies in 480 and 479. The last episode Herodotus records in his *Histories* brings the work to an appropriate close because it resolves the theme that has dominated more than half the narrative, that of Persia's attempts to establish boundaries of empire that supersede the boundaries of nature. In these last chapters Herodotus follows up on a story he had first mentioned in his account of Xerxes' bridge building (7.33), the punishment inflicted by the Greeks on a captured Persian general named Artayctes:

> Bringing him down to the headland where Xerxes bridged the strait (though some say it was to the hill above the city of Madytus), they nailed him to a plank and hung him up, and his son they stoned to death before his eyes. And having done that they sailed back to Greece, taking other property with them and in particular the ropes used to form

the bridges, intending to dedicate these in their temples. And nothing more happened during that year. (9.120–21)

There follows only a single paragraph, containing a flashback to the time of Cyrus, before the end of the text. Herodotus seems to have chosen the final undoing of the yoke between the continents and the offering up of its vanquished remnants to the gods of Greece as the terminus of a narrative that had no natural close (there were decades of Greco-Persian skirmishing still ahead). At the same moment he informs us, with a pointed reference to the controversy over the locale, that a high Persian commander in Europe was made to expiate the sins of his race on the very spot where Xerxes' bridges had once stood. Although some scholars have maintained that Herodotus died with the *Histories* still unfinished, one cannot imagine that he would have preferred any other endpoint to this one.

But while Herodotus assumed that the largest land masses, Europe and Asia, were destined to remain separate, he also noted that the earth's surface was subject to constant and inexorable change. Thus, whereas the Cnidians are forbidden to make a peninsula into an island, nature herself has within historical memory made a group of islands into a peninsula, by means of effluvial deposition (2.10). Over a far longer period, moreover, the river Nile has, according to Herodotus, filled in an immense gulf of sea with its sediments, thereby attaching the "peninsula" of Africa much more firmly to Asia; and he estimates that the same rate of deposition could entirely silt up the Red Sea over ten thousand years, were the Nile to be diverted in that direction. On the scale of geologic time, that is, natural forces alter the configuration of land and water on the planet's surface and even join continents: for one can infer from the discussion of the Nile in book 2 that one day the entire eastern Mediterranean will silt up, joining Asia, Africa, and

Europe into an enormous whole. Such speculations about on-going change in the geology of the continents reveal a different side of Herodotus's thinking from that discussed thus far, as does the surprising assertion, in a discussion of global geogra-phy, that "the earth is all one" and need not be divided into three parts under three different names (4.45). In passages like these one can see that the geographic scheme of the *Histories* is no more systematic or methodical than the moral and ethical framework discussed in the last chapter.

Indeed, in spite of the way in which Xerxes is condemned for forcing a bridge across the Hellespont, things do not always go ill for the Persians or for other nations when they alter phys-ical geography to exert political control. Herodotus may share some of Glendower's crusty conservatism, but he also finds much that is beneficial in technological progress and lists as *thōmata*, "wonders," some engineering feats he had observed in his travels or had heard about from others. He seems full of admiration, for example, when describing the public works that Queen Nitocris had undertaken for the city of Babylon, in-cluding an immense bridge over the Euphrates (1.186). And at one point, directly after the book 3 digression on the most dis-tant lands, he describes, again in admiring tones, the reservoir system by which the Persians extort revenue from the lands of central Asia. By damming up the waters of five rivers inside a ring of high mountains, the Persians compel their subjects to come to the royal palace at Susa and beg the king to irrigate their lands (3.117). Here Herodotus depicts a staggering vic-tory of technology over nature in the service of imperial power, but there is no imputation of *hybris* implied in his description, as we might have expected. Perhaps he regards the Persians' dominion over all of Asia as a more normal and natural state of affairs than their various attempts, under Cyrus, Darius, and

Xerxes, to invade Europe; by contrast, the yoking of continents is their great sin and invites retribution from the gods.

In the preface to this volume I compared Herodotus to the author of a medieval *mappamundi,* in that he saw the world whole and sought to depict it that way in his *Histories.* When he turns his attention to actual cartography, however, Herodotus seems closer in spirit to the Renaissance than to the Middle Ages, for he does not allow the myths inherited from high antiquity to influence his drawing of the world-map. Thus, whereas the creators of *mappaemundi* unfailingly showed the Garden of Eden in the farthest east, often with four great rivers spilling out of it as described in the Book of Genesis, Herodotus more closely resembles the Italian cartographer Fra Mauro, who in 1459 moved Paradise to an isolated corner of his world-map— outside the bounds of the earth itself. The places described in sacred scripture, Fra Mauro seems to have proclaimed, exist in a realm separate from the world defined by travel and exploration. Herodotus, in a similar way, cast aside the mythic world image established by Homer and Hesiod, turning instead to information gathered from travelers' reports and from firsthand research as a means of understanding the earth.

Herodotus's first step in this revision of the world-map was to banish the mythic river Ocean, a move as dramatic and revolutionary as Fra Mauro's handling of Paradise. For Ocean had been pictured over and over by Homer as a circular "river" surrounding the continents and had figured prominently in the thinking of the first Greek geographers, Anaximander and Hecataeus. To refute the existence of Ocean was to break, quite literally, the frame in which the ancient world picture was housed. Yet Herodotus asserts on several occasions that he does not believe in any such river and in fact regards it as a po-

etic fiction. For example, in describing his own version of the
world-map, as he does in chapters 37 through 45 of book 4, he
claims that "Europe is not clearly known by any one to be surrounded by water, either toward the east or the north" (4.45),
and elsewhere he makes the same claim in slightly different
terms: "I have not been able to learn of any eyewitness who
could attest that the further parts of Europe are bordered by
sea" (3.115). In one particularly sharp refutation, in response to
a fellow geographer who had made Ocean the source of the
river Nile, Herodotus writes,

> The man who discoursed about Ocean has carried this
> myth back into the unseen [that is, to a point beyond the
> reach of eyewitness investigation] and hence cannot be
> challenged by argument; for I myself do not know of the
> existence of any river Ocean, and I think that Homer or
> one of the other early poets invented the name and in-
> serted it into his poetry. (2.23)

In the course of refuting this unnamed geographic theorist,
who is quite likely Hecataeus of Miletus, Herodotus is forced
to call Homer a liar as well—all because he could find no firsthand confirmation that Europe was surrounded by sea.

By thus debunking Ocean, Herodotus abandoned the entire ancient conception of the earth's shape because this mythic
river had been thought, since Homer's time, to describe a per-
fect circle around the world's edge. In the introduction to his
discussion of the map, Herodotus leaves no doubt as to where
he stands on this question, openly scoffing at the ideas of his
forerunners:

> I laugh at those many people who draw maps of the earth,
> with none of them explaining things in a sensible manner;
> they draw Ocean flowing around the earth, which itself is

rounder than a circle drawn with a compass, and they make Asia and Europe the same size. (4.36)

Herodotus's principal target here seems, once again, to be Hecataeus of Miletus (whose geographic treatise came to be known under the title *Periodos Gēs*, or "Trip around the Earth," the same phrase that translates "map of the earth" in the sentence above). But the attack is also directed at the Ionian scientific tradition more broadly, which had preferred the mathematical purity of theoretical concepts to the messiness and complexity of the physical world. These Ionians, Herodotus implies, had adopted the fiction of Homer's Ocean because it suited their need for global symmetry, and they had then taken that symmetry a step further by dividing the circular earth into two neatly matching halves. Such abstraction appears ridiculous to an empiricist like Herodotus, who (as he goes on to explain) has come to know the earth as a bumpy and irregular place, the outer limits of which have not yet been entirely established.

Though he might scoff at the Ionians' neatly symmetrical world picture, however, Herodotus was deeply influenced by it in some of his own treatments of geographical questions. For instance, when he deals with the land of Egypt and the river Nile, in book 2 of the *Histories*, he assumes at several points that these stand in a symmetrical opposition to other lands and rivers across the Mediterranean. When he cannot say for certain what course the Nile follows south of the city of Elephantine, he assumes that it must run parallel to the river Ister (the Danube), the great stream whose mouth lies directly "opposite" (here meaning "due north of") the Nile delta (2.34). Not only the topography of Egypt, moreover, but the customs of its inhabitants have been organized by Herodotus along a North-South divide. He regards the Egyptians as a structural opposite

of European people, in the same way that he regards the Nile
as the opposite of the Ister:

> In Egypt, to the same degree that the climate there is dif-
> ferent and the river presents a different nature than other
> rivers, the inhabitants have established manners and cus-
> toms that are the opposite of other men in almost every re-
> spect. For among them the women go to market and do
> the buying and selling, while men stay home and weave.
> . . . Women urinate standing up, men sitting down. . . . In
> other places the priests of the gods let their hair grow,
> while in Egypt they shave it off. Whereas it is customary
> with others, during a time of mourning, for those most
> closely concerned with the loss to cut their hair, the Egyp-
> tians let their hair grow just after a death and let their
> beards grow, though otherwise clean-shaven. (2.35)

Such were the observations of a man who, despite his inclinations, had been conditioned to think of Egypt as "upside-down
land," based on the Ionian idea that Europe and Asia formed
opposing halves of the globe.

Even the image of a circular world-map, rejected so decisively by Herodotus in book 4, seems to be lurking in the background of the important book 3 passage we looked at above,
surveying the "furthest parts of the *oikeomenē*" and the riches
they produce. These outermost lands are said by Herodotus to
"surround and enclose the earth on all sides," exactly as the
river Ocean did for Homer and the Ionians. The very notion of
"furthest parts," moreover, seems out of tune with Herodotus's strenuous assertion elsewhere that the boundaries of the
earth cannot be determined in northern Europe and eastern
Asia.

Herodotus's cartography thus presents a paradox that
cannot be easily resolved: while spurning Ionian symmetrical

thinking at some points, he adopts that thinking at others without the least hint of dissatisfaction. Were the differing passages written at different stages of Herodotus's life and then left unreconciled by him when he came to put the *Histories* together? Or was he simply an unsystematic thinker who made use of an idea when it suited him but dropped it when it didn't? In either case, his work reveals why the title *Histories* fits it perhaps somewhat better than the other widely used alternative, *History*; as reflected in the plural form of the noun, its author's views of a single topic can be plural, divergent, or even, in a few extreme cases, contradictory of one another.

VII THE KINGDOM
OF CULTURE

Starting from his opening sentence, in which he promises to record "the great and wondrous deeds displayed by both Greeks and barbarians," Herodotus sets up a contrast in his *Histories* between Hellenic peoples and the others who surround them in all directions. Primarily by "barbarians" he means the Persians and their allies, and his first sentence looks forward to the second half of the text, in which his narrative cuts back and forth between the Persian capital or military camp and the leading cities or camps of the Greeks. But his exploration of the non-Greek world is also carried out in a different way in his first four books and includes not only the peoples of the Persian empire, comprising nearly all of Asia, but African tribes stretching far to the south and west of Egypt, Scythians and their kin ranging across the northeastern steppes, and the shadowy races of northern and western Europe reaching to the very shores of a dimly perceived Atlantic Ocean. In other words, Herodotus has included in his *Histories* a comprehensive map of humankind, matching in its scope the great world-map we examined in the previous chapter. And, just as he assigns a moral order to the structure of the world-map, so his studies of foreign races, or ethnographies as they are often called, reveal his thinking about the essential nature of humanity and the defining characteristics of what he refers to as *nomoi*—a plural word that can mean "laws," "customs," or "conventions" but that is often best translated as a singular, "culture."

It may seem obvious to us today that the Greeks possessed a single, common culture distinguishing them from the rest of the ancient world, but in Herodotus's time the awareness of this cultural identity had only recently taken shape. Earlier, in the Homeric poems for instance, the collective terms for "Greeks" (*Hellēnes*) and "non-Greeks" (*barbaroi*) do not appear, though the *Iliad* makes one passing reference to the linguistic gulf between the two sides: a people called Carians are referred to at one point as *barbarophōnoi*, "non-Greek-speakers." Otherwise, Homer ignores the language barrier in his account of the Trojan War (Achilles and Priam do not need interpreters to talk to each other) and portrays the Trojans as culturally indistinguishable from European Greeks: both worship the same gods, for instance, and use the same rites to bury their dead. In the centuries after Homer, however, as Greek colonists, merchants, and mercenaries came increasingly into contact with foreigners, cultural differences began to stand out in high relief, and chief among these a difference in language: the word *barbaros* emerges in the sixth century as a shorter version of Homer's *barbarophōnos*, meaning essentially "non-Greek-speaking." (One plausible etymology of the word traces it to a nonsense word, *barbar*, by which the Greeks imitated the sound of an unintelligible foreign tongue.) Also in the sixth century the word *Hellēnes* first appears as a collective name for Greek-speakers, merging for the first time the various racial, regional, and dialectical subgroups into which the Greeks had traditionally divided themselves: Ionians, Dorians, Achaeans, and the like. Thus both terms were still relatively new-coined at the time of the Persian invasions of Greece, and in fact those invasions seem to have done much to give them currency and to add the layering of moral value they would bear forever afterward: once Greeks had faced foreigners in a life-or-death struggle and soundly defeated them, they began to speak of *barbaroi* as peoples naturally or culturally inferior to themselves, not simply "non-Greek-speakers" but "barbarians" as well.

Though Herodotus chronicles the wars that many Greeks regarded as proof of their superiority over non-Greeks, he only rarely uses the word *barbaros* or the adjective derived from it in a negative sense. One such use has already been discussed: Herodotus, when referring to the insults hurled by Xerxes at the intractable Hellespont, castigates his words as "reckless and barbarian," applying the adjective *barbaros* to Asiatic moral qualities the Greeks found abhorrent. On another occasion Herodotus draws a less pejorative but still unflattering contrast between the intelligence levels of Greeks and *barbaroi*. He relates the story of how the tyrant Pisistratus used a stage trick to persuade the Athenians to take him back from exile, hiring a tall woman to impersonate the goddess Athena and drive him into the city in a chariot. Though he believes the story, Herodotus finds it ridiculous that the Athenians would fall for such a stunt because they were reputed to be the wisest of the Greeks, and the Greeks as a whole were the wisest of peoples: "From olden times the Greek race has been distinguished from the barbarian, both in its greater cleverness and its avoidance of silly simple-mindedness" (1.60). This blanket statement of Greek, and in particular Athenian, intellectual superiority sounds a bit odd in context, however; for only a few sentences earlier, Herodotus had asserted (in a passage whose meaning is far from clear) that the Athenian race is either descended from or intermixed with a people called Pelasgians, whom he identifies as *barbaroi* (1.57–58). Perhaps the two passages together reflect an assumption that the Athenian and Pelasgian peoples had long ago diverged into separate groups and that one of their distinctions was a difference in intelligence. But if this is the case, Herodotus would have a hard time explaining how that gap arose, in peoples descended from the same stock and living in the same location.

On these two occasions in the *Histories*, then, the qualities denoted by *barbaros* denote something morally or intellectually inferior to things Hellenic. But Herodotus elsewhere shows a remarkable evenhandedness in dealing with barbarian *nomoi* and in comparing them with those of the Greeks. Moreover, the problem he raises implicitly in his discussion of Athenian origins, that concerning the boundaries by which the categories of Greek and *barbaros* are marked off from one another, remains complex and open-ended throughout his work. In fact, Herodotus acknowledges at one point that the very word *barbaros* can be defined only in relative, not absolute, terms, that is, "alien" rather than "non-Greek." In relating an oracle given to the Egyptian pharaoh Necho that told him to stop building a canal because he was only paving the way for the *barbaros* (Darius) who would come after him, Herodotus notes that "the Egyptians call *barbaroi* all those who do not share their language" (2.158); the Greeks themselves, that is, are *barbaroi* when seen through Egyptian eyes. On one other occasion, Herodotus uses the word *Hellēn*, or "Greek," in a way that calls *its* meaning into question, mysteriously referring to a northern European tribe, the Kallipidae, as "Greek Scythians," that is, both Greeks and non-Greeks at the same time (4.17).

Indeed, at various other points in the *Histories* and particularly in his examination of Egypt, Herodotus detaches himself so thoroughly from a Hellenocentric point of view that a later Greek critic, the author of the treatise *On the Malice of Herodotus*, labeled him a *philobarbaros*, or "barbarian-lover." Though the charge made by the author of this treatise (usually identified as Plutarch) is certainly exaggerated and mean-spirited— it being the fate of broad-minded people throughout history to be branded as traitors by ultranationalists—one can understand how it arose: Herodotus *does* show an appreciation of foreign *nomoi* that is exceptional for his time and inspirational for ours. His credo of cultural tolerance is stated most clearly in a little anecdote appended to the story of Cambyses' occupation of Egypt in book 3. Gripped by insanity, Cambyses goes about insulting the religious rites of the Egyptians, even burning the images of their gods and breaking open tombs. Herodotus then comments,

> It is thus entirely clear to me that Cambyses had gone very much insane: for otherwise he would not have tried to mock at sacred and customary matters. For if one were to bid all of humankind to choose the best customs from among all customs, after surveying the field each would choose their own. . . . That all peoples believe in this way about customs can be judged from many indications, and in particular from the following: Darius, when he was king, summoned the Greeks who were with him and asked at what price they would be willing to eat their dead fathers; they said that there was nothing for which they would do that. After that Darius called the Indians known as Kallatians, who eat their parents, and, while the Greeks stood by and learned through an interpreter what was said, asked at what price they would agree to burn their dead fathers with fire; they cried aloud and demanded that he not speak such blasphemy. These things have been established by custom, and Pindar seems to me to have said rightly in his poetry, "Custom is the king of all." (3.38)

The strength of his beliefs about the relative value of *nomoi* here moves Herodotus to a rare quotation from poetry—though he has either misremembered or distorted the original sense of the little tag line from Pindar, and his use of it in the present context is far from clear.

One possible and highly attractive reading of Herodotus's train of thought in the above passage is, "Since all human practices are determined by custom, none can be judged as morally superior to any other." Herodotus himself refrains from making such judgments throughout the *Histories*, even when reporting practices that would have seemed abhorrent to most Greek observers. For example, the very words he uses above in connection with Indian necrophagy, "These things have been established by custom," recur in a passage in which he describes in detail—and in entirely neutral tones—how a Scythian warrior dismembers his dead enemy, using the scalp to make a coat, the skin of the hand (nails and all) for a quiver-lid, and the skull for a drinking-cup (4.64–65). Elsewhere he reports such practices as cannibalism, polygamy, and extreme sexual promiscuity without the slightest hint of distaste or moral disapproval. On only one occasion does Herodotus openly condemn a foreign practice, calling "most shameful" the Babylonian custom of ritual female prostitution in honor of the goddess known as Mylitta (1.199). Evidently the intrusion of sexuality into religious worship was more than even he could accept with equanimity: on another occasion he voices displeasure at the idea that most nations, Greeks and Egyptians excepted, permit intercourse in sacred shrines or allow worshipers to enter without being ritually cleansed after sex (2.64).

But Herodotus's metaphor above of the marketplace in which each nation chooses its own *nomoi* suggests a different and more problematic sense in which "Custom is the king of all." If we understand this to mean that Custom acts as ruler and lawgiver, establishing a code of behavior that each nation invariably follows, then Herodotus's statement here is belied by his own account of the Persians in book 1, who, as he tells us, "adopt foreign customs more than any other men" (1.135). For example, the Persians don Median dress when they find it better looking than their own, imitate the armor of the Egyptians, and from the Greeks learn (as Herodotus notes without comment) the practice of pederasty. Furthermore, the Greeks, as Herodotus relates at some length in book 2, have adopted large segments of *their* culture from the Egyptians, including (as we shall see in a moment) the names and cult practices of their gods; and Herodotus even raises the possibility that the Egyptians, though in most respects resistant to foreign *nomoi*, have themselves learned the practice of circumcision from the Ethiopians (2.104). When one looks closely at the ethnographic sections of the *Histories*, one finds that the boundaries of culture are considerably more porous and the question of propriety more complicated than Herodotus indicates with his metaphor of a cultural marketplace. In fact, nearly all the peoples on Herodotus's world-map, to one degree or another, shop around for the *nomoi* they find most useful or pleasurable. In general, the nations near the center of the world, that is, in the bustling heart of the "market," do this more easily, while those at the perimeter remain more isolated and impermeable: the Scythians, for example, put to death one of their rulers for attempting to import the worship of Dionysus from the Greeks (4.77–80), whereas the Greeks had earlier taken over the very same worship from the Egyptians, seemingly without difficulty (2.49). But Herodotus's cultural marketplace at times seems governed by no pattern at all, with *nomoi* being traded in every direction at once. The westernmost tribes of Libya have in one case adopted the use of helmets and shields *from* the Greeks, yet in another have given *to* the Greeks a different piece of armor, the aegis, or goatskin shield, carried by

Athena (4.180, 189). If there is some King Custom presiding over any of these nations, he seems to do very little to protect his borders.

The question of cultural autonomy in the *Histories* becomes most pressing in the case of Hellenism, and here Herodotus shows a remarkable willingness to point out foreign or "barbarian" elements in his own culture. Egypt, above all, is identified in book 2 as the source of many central Greek practices; indeed, the "Egyptification" of Greece, particularly in matters of religion, forms a major theme of book 2, and this mightily galls the author of *On the Malice of Herodotus*, who sees it as conclusive evidence of philobarbarism. Modern readers, too, may be surprised to find Herodotus willing to derive the "names" of many Greek gods, by which he appears to mean their entire identities, from Egypt; still other such "names" he traces to sources among the Pelasgians (the pre-Greek inhabitants of the Aegean) and the Libyans, claiming none as original to the Hellenes themselves. Herodotus here operates from two assumptions that represent an extreme version of what a modern-day anthropologist would call diffusionism: first, he believes, on the basis of superficial resemblances, that the divinities of foreign cultures are the same as those of the Greeks, although they go under different names (so that Egyptian Isis translates to Greek Demeter, Osiris to Dionysus, Ptah to Hephaestus, and so on); second, he insists that whenever a custom in one part of the world resembles another elsewhere, the older one must be the source of the more recent. And since the Egyptians belong to the very oldest stratum of human society, dating back some seventeen thousand years according to their own estimate, Herodotus credits them with having originated all foreign *nomoi* that resemble their own. By the same token the Egyptians take over few *nomoi* from the outside, and in particular none from the Greeks; this ancient civilization has nothing to learn from its juniors, so culture flows in one direction only, as Herodotus resolutely asserts in a discussion of Dionysiac worship: "I will always deny that the Egyptians got this rite from the Greeks, or any other aspect of culture" (2.49).

In all this, Herodotus, remarkably enough, seems neither to have felt any threat to his own national pride, nor to have taken steps to deflect any that might be felt by his audience. It is clear that his visit (or visits) to Egypt had made a deep impression on him, in perhaps the same way that a passage to India has transformed many modern westerners: he found there not only a vastly old society but one steeped in piety and mysticism, indeed "the most extraordinarily devoted to the gods of all mankind" (2.37; the adverb used here is given a pejorative tone in some translations, "excessively" rather than "extraordinarily," but the Greek word need not imply disapproval). Beyond religious matters, moreover, the scale of Egyptian monuments and works of engineering utterly astounded Herodotus, as their remains did nineteenth-century Europeans when Napoleon's invasion reintroduced them to the Western world (a culture shock still reverberating today). The prevalence in Egypt of wonders and of "works greater than speech can tell" leads Herodotus to proclaim, early in book 2, that he will say more about that country than any other, and he goes on to fulfill his promise by creating a masterful, compelling, and highly detailed portrait of this strange "down under" civilization. Whether or not he composed this book as a separate work and later spliced it into the *Histories*, his tone throughout is that of a man under the spell of an exotic alien culture, so much so that he can even seem disappointed by the shorter history or more meager accomplishments of his own.

If it was madness on the part of Cambyses to mock at Egyptian religion, then Herodotus's attitude throughout book 2 seems the ultimate form of sanity.

But Herodotus's humane relativism is not an inevitable or universally shared attitude toward culture, within the world of the *Histories*. At the opposite end of the tolerance spectrum stand the Persians, who, in Herodotus's eyes, look out at the rest of the world with a crude kind of ethnic self-righteousness:

> After themselves, they honor those dwelling nearest to them, and next those dwelling next, and thus they proceed in degrees of honor; least of all they hold in honor those dwelling furthest away, thinking that they themselves are by far the best of men in every respect, and that the others have a proportionately lesser share of virtue, and that those dwelling furthest away from themselves are the basest. (1.134)

Such an attitude not only conflicts directly with the idea that "Custom is king," as formulated by Herodotus, but also ignores the fact (mentioned only a few sentences after the one just quoted) that the Persians themselves eagerly adopt the practices of the foreigners they look down upon. In light of this information, the Persian sense of cultural superiority begins to seem mere chauvinism, the ethnologic concomitant of their program of world conquest. It does them little credit, for example, that even Greece, a nation lying near the edge of the Persians' world-map and therefore presumably subject to their contempt, has contributed a rather inglorious but important element to their culture, the practice of pederasty.

The Persians' haughtiness toward foreign *nomoi* gets directed toward the Greeks on several occasions in the *Histories*, beginning with a passage that closely precedes the description of Persian ethnocentrism just discussed. In describing Persian eating habits, Herodotus observes,

> They eat few main courses, but many desserts, served at intervals; and on account of this the Persians say that the

Greeks stop eating while still hungry, since nothing much is served to them after the main meal; and they say that if anything *were* served, the Greeks would never stop eating (1.133).

A similar but harsher comparison is made later in book 1, after Cyrus has consolidated his empire and has revealed his aggressive designs on the Greek cities of Anatolia. The Spartans send an envoy to Cyrus bidding him not to harm any of those cities and are insulted for their troubles:

> It is said that Cyrus asked those present who these Spartans were among the Greeks, and what strength of numbers they possessed so as to make such proclamations to him. When he found out, he said to the Spartan envoy: "I've never been afraid of men such as you, who have a place set aside in the center of the city where they gather together and, by taking vows of honesty, cheat one another. If I stay in health they will have cause to talk not about Ionian troubles, but their own." Cyrus cast these words in the teeth of all the Greeks, since they have set up marketplaces where they buy and sell; whereas the Persians themselves make no use of marketplaces, nor do they have any public market anywhere. (1.153)

Both these passages illustrate the kind of cultural self-satisfaction associated with modern stereotypes of the ugly American, the type of traveler who, in rural Greece, for instance, will (in an ironic reversal of Cyrus's insult) complain of the difficulty of finding supermarkets and department stores. The second passage, moreover, reveals how closely this attitude is tied to military expansionism, in that Cyrus's contempt for the Hellenic way of life leads him to contemplate an attack not just on Ionia but on European Greece as well. The first faint glimmer in the *Histories* of the coming intercontinental conflict is thus generated, significantly enough, during a moment of Persian cultural arrogance and closed-mindedness; and Herodotus's narrative of the conflict itself will develop such moments into a major theme of his work.

Not only the Persians' impulse to attack foreign peoples, but also their ability to rule them is associated by Herodotus with their sense of cultural dominion: just as he shows the Persians controlling the rivers of Asia in order to subdue their subjects, so he also shows them manipulating the continent's *nomoi*. Thus when the conquered Lydians, in book 1, threaten to revolt and throw off the Persian yoke, Cyrus asks their former leader Croesus how to deal with the situation. Croesus fears that Cyrus has in mind the wholesale destruction of Lydia, and so offers him a less drastic alternative:

> "Forgive the Lydians, and, so that they will not revolt or cause you trouble, order them as follows: send a message forbidding them to have weapons of war and order them to put on soft tunics beneath their clothes and to wear slippers, and command them to learn to play the lyre and the harp and to teach their children to tend shops. Soon, sire, you will see that they've become women instead of men, so as to cause you no further worries about rebellion." . . . Cyrus was delighted by this advice and let go of his anger, declaring that he agreed. (1.155–56)

For Herodotus's contemporaries this anecdote would have particular point because the Lydians of their day were considered a slack, effeminate people excessively fond of luxury and soft music. The Persians, that is, here bring about a permanent transformation of the Lydians' character simply by imposing new *nomoi* upon them (and Herodotus anticipates the theories of modern-day behavioralists in presuming that such transformation is possible). Cyrus, who in the episode just before this had revealed his contempt for Greek mercantilism, here seizes the opportunity to enfeeble his subjects by turning them into a nation of shopkeepers; he makes custom the "king of all things" in a more literal sense than Herodotus intended in his quote from Pindar.

But the most telling demonstrations of the link between ethnocentrism and imperialism come in Herodotus's accounts of Persian wars against primitive or tribal peoples, in particular the Massagetae of book 1, the Ethiopians of book 3, and the Scythians of book 4. In all three of these wars the Persians cross the boundaries of Asia to fight in other continents, as we have seen; and in all three cases they also cross into a cultural zone very different from their own, so that the conflict that ensues becomes a confrontation between differing sets of *nomoi*. And all three times the Persians meet with failure, as their self-aggrandizing view of the world and their lack of regard for distant races lead them into reckless diplomatic and military blunders.

Herodotus depicts both the Massagetae and the Scythians as nomadic peoples, belonging to a belt of such peoples that surrounds the earth's central region of agriculture, technology, and urbanization. That is to say, Herodotus, like the Persians, arranges the cultures of the world in concentric circles, though based on levels of development rather than moral value: as he moves outward on an anthropological "map" he also moves backward in time, finding peoples that are increasingly more primitive in terms of social organization, material culture, and technological progress. Thus the nomadic races of the hinterlands stand about as far apart, in cultural terms, from Greeks and Persians as North America's native tribes did from the first European settlers. Beyond these nomadic peoples lie other races still more primitive, such as the Androphagi, who eat human flesh (4.106); and beyond these, at the outermost edge of the world, humanity becomes so primitive as to be godlike in its natural purity.

When Cyrus attacks the Massagetae, he elects, acting once again on the advice of Croesus, to use their primitivism as a way to subvert them. Knowing that the Massagetae are unfamiliar with delicate foods and in particular with wine, Cyrus contrives that a rich banquet table laden with these things will fall into the hands of their chief warriors; after these men have eaten and drunk themselves into a stupor, Cyrus attacks and kills them and captures Spargapises, the son of the Massagetan queen Tomyris. The use of wine in this stratagem is particularly interesting because Herodotus has earlier informed us that the Persians themselves are great wine-drinkers and in fact use wine to gain clarity when they make important state decisions (1.133). Persian culture, that is, has habituated them to this most sophisticated and civilized of beverages, so that they can turn wine into a weapon against a people innocent of its effects. Readers may be reminded of a similar stratagem practiced by Odysseus against the Cyclops in Homer's *Odyssey*— or, closer to our own times, the way in which native American tribes were debilitated and demoralized by their first taste of European firewater.

The message Queen Tomyris sends to Cyrus in response to the capture of her son—a message that should be regarded as the composition of Herodotus, who could not have known what was really said in such a distant place, long before his birth— shows her perplexity over the nature of this new weapon; she refers to it contemptuously as "that vine-grown fruit, with which you fill yourselves and then become so maddened that evil words rise up in you as the wine goes down" (1.212). She also expresses outrage at the Persian decision to fight by trickery rather than main force, charging Cyrus with *katubrisas*, "committing a vicious act of *hybris*," against her troops—her wrath prompting her to use a powerful compound verb found nowhere else in the *Histories*. That is, Cyrus's use of wine, a product of his more advanced civilization, to subvert a primitive people appears to the Massagetae to be a moral atrocity and incenses them to fight even more fiercely and resolutely than before. When Tomyris later defeats Cyrus and stuffs the head of his corpse into a wineskin filled with blood, we are left with the clear implication that his form of cross-cultural warfare has backfired and that he has received poetic justice for his *hybris*, being forced symbolically to drink his fill of blood to atone for the drink he so treacherously served the Massagetae. (One is reminded of the revenge that Aztec warriors were said to have taken on captured conquistadors: to glut their incomprehensible appetite for gold, the Aztecs allegedly poured that metal, molten, down their throats.)

Following this initial Persian defeat at the hands of the nomads beyond their borders, Herodotus stages a different type of cultural confrontation in book 3, when Cambyses attacks an African tribe called the Long-lived Ethiopians. These Ethiopians live by the shores of what Herodotus terms "the southern sea," that is, at the furthest edge of the inhabited world, and thus belong to the set of peoples who (as we saw in the previous chapter) are blessed with the richest resources of the earth. However, the world's outer perimeter also contains its most primitive stratum of culture, according to the different but related scheme in which Herodotean peoples grow less advanced as one moves away from the earth's center. At first glance the two conceptions may seem to be in conflict given that in our own day we tend to associate cultural primitivism with material poverty, but a closer look reveals how easily they coexist: the rim peoples possess the greatest natural riches but require only the most elemental skills to harvest them; they are hunter-gatherers who pick up gold and amber off the ground rather than nuts and berries. The Ethiopians, for example, eat boiled meats from a kind of limitless buffet called the Table of the Sun; they owe their tribal epithet, Long-lived, to the miraculous, violet-scented springs in which they bathe, waters that (as Herodotus believes) keep them alive to the age of 120 or even longer. These are not merely noble savages, but human beings living in such an idealized state of nature as to be akin to gods. In fact, Herodotus's audience would doubtless have associated these Ethiopians with the ones described by Homer in the *Iliad* and *Odyssey*, a people who play host to Zeus and the other Olympians at fabulous feasts and banquets.

Like Cyrus before him, Cambyses attempts to gain the upper hand over this distant race by using his cultural "superiority" as a tactical advantage. He sends envoys to the court of the Ethiopian king, ostensibly to present him with finely wrought gifts—gold jewelry, dyed clothing, incense, and wine—but with the hidden purpose of spying on his future adversary. The king, a proud tribal warrior of great strength and beauty, immediately sees through this subterfuge and sends back a scornful rejoinder to Cambyses, upbraiding him for unjustly seeking to attack those who have done him no wrong. He then turns a haughty eye upon the Persian gifts, commenting on each in turn in a scene that Herodotus records in close detail. Although he encounters them for the first time, the most precious products of the technological world do not evoke wonder or delight from this godlike being, as the iron bells and glass beads carried by Columbus's crew did from the Caribbean natives they encountered. Rather, the Ethiopian treats these trinkets with scorn and disdain: the dyed robes, for example, strike him as evidence of the duplicitousness of the Persians, for why else would anyone give to cloth a color not its own? Only the wine wins praise from the Ethiopian king, who admits that in this one item his own culture has been surpassed by that of the Persians, and the exception is an important one, given what we have seen of wine's significance in Cyrus's Massagetan campaign. The king seems to regard this drink not as an intoxicant, however, but as a tonic for preserving health and extending life; a Long-lived Ethiopian to the core, he brings the wine into his own cultural framework in a way that the Massagetae do not.

When the spies report back to headquarters and Cambyses learns how little his gifts are esteemed by his foe, he instantly becomes "insane and distracted," according to Herodotus, and leads his army off toward the Ethiopians without pausing to make adequate provisions; much of the expedition thus perishes of hunger, driven onward by its mad commander. It seems the Persians, who on other occasions show little respect for *nomoi* different from their own, cannot endure to have their *nomoi* looked down on by others, and this militant nationalism leads them into self-destruction. Indeed, Herodotus seems to have very purposefully brought these Ethiopians into his narrative (they are otherwise unknown to history) to deliver a rebuke to Persian cultural smugness: they stand as the ultimate counterargument to the ethnocentric worldview that sees the peoples at the earth's edge as its basest, most contemptible races.

If in book 3 Herodotus thus explores the ideal cultural condition of the earth's rim, in book 4 he returns to the more rugged zone of nomadism just inside that outer perimeter, examining first the tribes of Scythia, the region north of the Black Sea, and then those of Libya, or western Africa. Here his landscapes are broad and barren, containing neither the natural wonders of Ethiopia and other furthest lands, nor the manmade marvels of central cultures like Egypt; in fact, Herodotus remarks at one point, as if disappointed in the lack of technological development among the nomads, that "near the Black Sea . . . one finds the most ignorant peoples, except for the Scythians, of any region" (4.46). But he remains interested even when unimpressed and gives thumbnail sketches of each tribe in turn, including information about its diet, clothing, religion, language, and sexual practices. These rapid-fire mini-ethnographies have made book 4 a favorite not only among anthropologists but among all students of the human condition; the roll call of nomadic *nomoi* creates a sense of the immense diversity of human life, in particular the many brave and clever ways by which our species adapts to tough environments. Where neither nature nor culture offer an easy living, there human resourcefulness most compellingly reveals itself:

> Because the Scythian land is dreadfully short of wood, the inhabitants have contrived the following for boiling their meat: when they cut up a sacrificial animal, they take the meat clean off the bones; this they throw into native cauldrons, if they happen to have any . . . and boil it by making a fire of the animal's bones. If they have no cauldron to hand, they put all the meat inside the animal's stomach, add water, and start a fire from the bones. For the bones burn beautifully, and the stomach easily contains the meat taken off of them; and in this way an ox cooks itself, or any other sacrificial animal. (4.61)

Beyond its intrinsic interest as anthropological lore, however, Herodotus's portrait of nomadic life in book 4 becomes crucial to his larger theme of cross-cultural confrontation when the Persians under Darius mount an invasion of Scythia (chapters 83–142). Lacking the superhuman powers or magical wealth of the Ethiopians, the Scythians face a tough fight against the more numerous and better organized Persians. But they can still rely upon what Herodotus elaborately praises as "the one greatest and most cleverly devised of all human affairs we have ever seen," their very nomadism: "They have no towns or fortified walls, but carry their houses with them and can shoot arrows from horseback; their sustenance is not from farmland but from herds, and their houses are atop carts; so how could they be anything but unconquerable and impossible to approach?" (4.46). The course of the war that follows justifies Herodotus's enthusiasm: the Scythians, retreating before the Persian advance, utterly confound Darius by leaving him no target to attack; when the Persians attempt to engage in "civilized" warfare by building a series of fortifications from which to mount sallies, the Scythians simply desert the area and render the forts useless. Herodotus has here constructed a war that embodies in action the differing *nomoi* of its combatants: the builders of cities and palaces find their technology defeated by the run-and-hide tactics of the roving nomads. The Persians, anticipating the modern-day failures of professional armies to defeat ragtag guerrillas in their native terrain, eventually give up chasing the enemy and return home, dishonored if not defeated.

Throughout his first four books, then, Herodotus puts the Persians through a kind of steeplechase of cultural confrontations, showing in three prominent episodes how their inability to understand or appreciate foreign *nomoi* causes them to underestimate their opponents and put themselves at risk. He constructs all three, moreover, as struggles between a technologically advanced society on the one hand and various stages of primitivism on the other, and this contrast will again be important in the second half of the text; for the wars of Darius and Xerxes against the Greeks will once again pit the Persians against a people they regard as backward and unsophisticated, yet who prove to be their betters on the field of battle. Indeed, Herodotus calls our attention back to the episodes we have just

surveyed at the beginning of book 7, when Xerxes first contemplates his invasion of Greece: his uncle Artabanus, attempting to dissuade him, says, "I remember how the expedition of
Cyrus against the Massagetae fared; I remember also that of
Cambyses against the Ethiopians; and I myself went along
with Darius on his campaign against the Scythians" (7.18). In
the three failed invasions of books 1, 3, and 4, as in the life stories of the three monarchs who led them, Herodotus has established the patterns that will underlie everything that happens
from book 5 onward.

VIII THE ART OF THE STORYTELLER

ANY WRITER OF HISTORY MUST ALSO BE, TO SOME DEGREE, THE teller of a story; indeed, the word "story" originated as an abbreviated form of "history," and the two words remain fused in Italian *storia* and French *histoire*. For Herodotus, the history of the Greek conflict with Persia was, among other things, a great story: it had colorful, exotic scenery, larger-than-life characters, thrilling action, and an ending that, at the time it actually occurred at least, had come as an enormous surprise. What is more, this vast and sweeping story gave room for the inclusion of dozens of smaller tales, some no more than a sentence or two in length, others occupying many pages of Greek text, some intimately connected to the main "plot line," others so distant from it as to be no more than footnotes or parentheses. These shorter tales reveal a side of Herodotus's work that has captivated its readers from the first—or perhaps "listeners" would be more accurate, as we shall see in a moment. The *Histories* preserves within the tapestry of its main narrative an assortment of the most lively, cleverest, strangest, and sexiest stories of its day, tales worthy of Chaucer's *Canterbury Tales* or Boccaccio's *Decameron*, and all selected and retold by a master of the storytelling art.

The word "story" also carries a somewhat different connotation in the field of journalism, and in this sense, too, it applies to the tales of the *Histories*. When newspaper reporters say, for example, that a certain event makes a great story, they mean not only that they can generate articles from it, but that its oddity, its emotional impact, or the larger truths that it captures make it an object of fascination to an entire society. Above all, it is *novelty* that attracts us to such "news" stories: we are irresistibly drawn to the spectacle of things never seen before or things done on a bigger or more extreme scale than ever. Although Herodotus's concerns in the *Histories* go far beyond those of a journalist, he shares the newsman's passion for the great story, the event that captures the mind and expands the limits of experience. Time and again he refers to individuals as "the first we know of" to have done something and to events as "the greatest we know of," "the only time we know of," and so on. These expressions have led one recent writer to compare Herodotus's text, in this one aspect, to the *Guinness Book of World Records*, in that both preserve the most extraordinary and extreme human achievements of their day. It's a suggestive analogy but needs to be qualified in this way: for Herodotus, as for the best journalists, firsts and mosts are not significant simply because they are record-breakers, but because of the insights they offer into human life or even the natural and divine worlds surrounding it.

Let us take as an example of this greatest-ever type of story the tale of Hermotimus the Pedasian in book 8. This story is inserted into the *Histories*, like many others, as a kind of footnote to the larger narrative: after the battle of Salamis, when Xerxes has decided to return to Persia, he also sends his children home, under the guardianship of one Hermotimus. It was this Hermotimus, as Herodotus says, whose injuries received the greatest retribution, or *tisis*, of any one known to him. Earlier in his life he had been castrated and sold into slavery by a marketer of eunuchs, a Chian Greek named Panionius. But he had the good fortune to end up at the court of the Persian king, where he became Xerxes' favorite and most trusted eunuch.

Having been sent on some business for Xerxes into the lands around Chios, Hermotimus happens to bump into his castrator, Panionius:

> Recognizing Panionius, Hermotimus spoke many friendly words to him, recounting first of all how many good things he had gotten on account of Panionius and then promising to do him equal good in exchange for this, if he would bring his household there to live. Panionius received these words gladly and brought his wife and children. So, when Hermotimus had got him and his family entrapped, he spoke as follows: "You who get your livelihood from the most unholy pursuit of all mankind, what wrong did I or any of my kin do, either to you or to any of your kin, that you turned me into a nothing instead of a man? You thought that what you did then would go unnoticed by the gods, but they, according to their just law, have brought you, after your unholy deeds, into my hands—so that you won't complain of the punishment coming to you from me." After Hermotimus thus reviled him, the children were brought in, and Panionius was compelled to cut off the privates of his own children, of whom there were four, and under compulsion he did this; then, when he was finished, his sons, under compulsion, cut his off too. So, in this way did *tisis* and Hermotimus catch up to Panionius. (8.106)

This gruesome little revenge drama has almost no explicit relevance to its context, the aftermath of the battle of Salamis, and Hermotimus does not figure into the historical narrative in any larger way (he never appears again in the *Histories*). But his story struck Herodotus as something worthy of inclusion, for a number of reasons. For one thing, as any fan of modern-day crime dramas can attest, the spectacle of evildoers getting paid back for their crimes is intensely exciting and pleasurable. Herodotus quite obviously wants us to savor this pleasure: after setting the stage for the revenge, he suspends the action to give Hermotimus a thrilling reproach-speech, simultaneously righteous and mildly sadistic in tone (its final clause, "so that you won't complain . . . ," drips with vicious irony). The tale succeeds at the level of pure, visceral entertainment, therefore, and Herodotus was certainly interested in it for that reason. But beyond that, he has given it a larger point in his concluding sentence, "In this way did *tisis* and Hermotimus catch up to Panionius." Here Herodotus comes close to personifying *tisis*, the retributive principle that, as we have seen, helps bring about the fall of Croesus and other instances of payback in the *Histories*. He thus gives his assent to the moral Hermotimus himself draws from his remarkable revenge, that "the gods . . . *according to their just law*, have brought you into my hands" (emphasis added). In this way a story that Herodotus introduces seemingly as a sidelight, a mere addition to his collection of greatest evers, turns out to have a larger ethical and even theological significance within the context of the *Histories*.

Few of the stories Herodotus weaves into the fabric of his narrative can be capped by such a clear moral, however, and in many cases fierce debates have arisen over how or whether these inwoven tales relate to the larger tapestry. The first and most memorable example of this kind of controversial tale comes near the beginning of book 1, where the story of Arion and the dolphin suddenly begins—so suddenly that many readers find themselves immersed in the story without entirely knowing how they got there— after an account of the war between King Alyattes of Lydia and the Greek city of Miletus. Herodotus had earlier reported that the tyrant Periander of Corinth played a part in ending this war by informing Thrasybulus, tyrant of Miletus, about an oracle unfavorable to the

Lydians' side. What might have been only brief, incidental mention of Periander, however, reminds Herodotus of another greatest ever: this Periander, as the Corinthians say, had experienced the greatest wonder of his time, when Arion was carried on the back of a dolphin (1.23). It seems that Arion, the best lyre player and singer of his day, was sailing home to Corinth from Italy, where he had made a lot of money performing his music. Far out at sea, the Corinthian sailors conducting his ship took his money and gave him the choice of killing himself there on shipboard or leaping to a seemingly certain death in the sea. Over the side Arion went, in full "concert dress," bravely singing a hymn in honor of Apollo—when suddenly a dolphin appeared, took him on its back, and carried him all the way to Tainaron on the Greek mainland. Safely landed, Arion made his way to Corinth and told the tyrant there, Periander, what had happened. Periander doubted his story but kept the musician at court until the sailors arrived; when he questioned these men about Arion and they claimed to have left him safe and sound back in Italy, Arion jumped out of hiding to give them the lie.

After bringing this story to its gratifying conclusion, Herodotus briefly notes the existence of a bronze statue at Tainaron showing Arion riding the dolphin and then resumes the larger narrative just where he had left off: "Alyattes the Lydian carried on the war against the Milesians and then died, having reigned for 57 years." No effort is made, as in the case of the Hermotimus story, to close with some suggestion about the meaning or relevance of Arion's redemption, unless we suppose (as at least one scholar has done) that the entire story merely explains the existence of the odd-looking Tainaron statue. Naturally, questions have arisen as to what the Arion story is doing here and what Herodotus wants us to make of it. Is it important that Arion gets rescued while singing a hymn to

Apollo because, in the episode to which this story is attached, Miletus and Lydia resolve their conflict thanks to an oracle from Apollo? That is, should the story be read not as an artless digression from, but a meaningful juxtaposition with, events in the surrounding narrative? Or should it be connected with a series of stories about Periander and his father, Cypselus, a series that continues in books 3 and 5 and thus forms one of the running subplots that tie the *Histories* together? Or should we look even farther afield, as one recent writer has done, by connecting Arion's leap with other "brave gestures" performed by human beings unbowed in the face of death—a set of stories scattered widely throughout the entire length of the *Histories?* Or are all these links only illusory and the placement of the Arion tale simply a question of expediency: Herodotus had a great story to tell and as soon as the opportunity arose, with the first mention of Periander, he seized it?

This last possibility is the one that most urgently needs to be addressed because it implies that Herodotus did not select his digressive tales or include them at particular points in his narrative with any intention other than to entertain. His technique would be like that of a rambling lecturer who periodically interrupts a talk to say, "That reminds me of a story." In fact, this is exactly how Herodotus was long thought to have operated, and some scholars today continue to see him not as a writer, but as a public speaker, who sought to spice up his lectures by seasoning them with colorful anecdotes. The evidence supporting this notion is inconclusive, and the whole question remains unresolved, but in the absence of such resolution, it seems a mistake to think of the *Histories,* which everywhere has the feel of a unified, coherent work, as anything other than a book, composed by an author who conceived of it as a whole and expected his audience to do the same. By the same token, it would be a mistake to dismiss the stories of the

Histories, even those like Arion and the dolphin that seem spliced in without regard to context, as mere crowd pleasers designed to focus the attention of listeners. After all, much of the jesting and byplay of Shakespearean drama was once understood primarily as a diversion for the groundlings among the audience—an assumption that obscured what are now seen as important connections to the plays' main themes.

Of course, one can go too far in the other direction as well, by ignoring the degree to which Herodotus does use stories to entertain. Even though (as I believe) he did think of himself as primarily a writer, not a lecturer, he often commences a long episode of the *Histories* with a particularly gripping anecdote, much as a public speaker today might warm up his audience with a joke. In fact, the work as a whole starts out in just this way, immediately after Herodotus has announced his theme and chosen his starting point. The story of Candaules, the king who "fell passionately in love with his own wife" (1.8), and his bodyguard Gyges provides important background to the fall of Croesus four generations later, but also, undeniably, draws the reader into the narrative with a still-irresistible combination of illicit eroticism and violent crime. Obviously, Herodotus himself enjoyed such material immensely and expected his audience to do so as well. To revert to the analogy drawn earlier between Herodotean storytelling and modern-day journalism, one can more easily picture the stories of the *Histories* appearing in a scandal-sheet tabloid than in a more austere and high-minded newspaper like the *Wall Street Journal.*

The world in which Herodotus lived, of course, had no newspapers or any other form of mass written communication. Though the alphabet had been in use for more than two centuries before Herodotus's birth, and many Greeks could no doubt write their names or make out short inscriptions, the skills required to read long literary texts were, probably throughout the fifth century, restricted to a small minority; and as a result the books available for them to read were few as well. Thus, although literacy in the most basic sense was already widespread in Herodotus's day, Greece as yet remained an oral culture, in the sense that most people got most of their information and certainly nearly all of their stories about the past by word of mouth. Indeed, the process of *historiē*, or "research," by which Herodotus produced the *Histories* must have consisted largely of listening to people, both Greek and foreign, tell their stories. Herodotus knew the value of written sources, of course, and on a few occasions he brings them to bear on his subject; in one case (his account of the tribute-list of Darius, 3.89–96), he seems to be working directly from Persian government records, probably after having them translated into Greek. Still, Herodotus shows far less interest in such documentary evidence than he might have, and certainly a good deal less than any of his successors.

We must never lose sight, when reading stories in the *Histories* like that of Arion and the dolphin, of the crucial boundary between Herodotus's oral culture and later, literate ages like our own. Though we can never fully cross back over the line and reenter our lost oral past, we must at least try to understand that past on its own terms, which means treating Herodotus's stories as a vital and important part of his work rather than as mere seasoning or spice. Herodotus expresses his meanings in stories because stories were the common currency of the culture in which he lived; one might say that he *thinks* in stories, just as a modern writer thinks in paragraphs or chapters.

A good illustration of this primacy of storytelling comes in Herodotus's depiction of a Spartan policy debate in book 5. The Spartans have at this point decided to restore the tyrant Hippias to power in Athens, and they have summoned their allies to an assembly to inform them of this course. A Corinthian ambassador, Sosicles by name (or Socles in some versions of the text), speaks in opposition, claiming that tyrannical government in its very nature leads to abuse of power and criminality. Because the Spartans themselves have no direct experience of this form of government, Sosicles offers to tell them of the excesses committed in his own city by two powerful tyrants, Cypselus and his son, Periander. At this point his speech begins to transform itself into a story as he describes how Cypselus's coming to power was foretold by an oracle; how the government at Corinth tried to have him killed as an infant, and how the assassins found themselves unable to murder so charming a baby; how his mother, fearing a second attack, hid the baby in a storage box; and how Cypselus grew up and came to power, emboldened by the prediction of another oracle that he and his children, but not his grandchildren, would rule in Corinth. All this material—already more lengthy than any other speech in the *Histories*—only forms the prelude to Sosicles' main point, namely, the crimes committed by Cypselus and his son, Periander. Even here, Sosicles bypasses the most historically relevant facts about the tyranny and instead focuses at length on a single lurid episode, in which Periander has intercourse with the body of his dead wife, Melissa, and is then tormented by her ghost. When Sosicles finishes at last, his audience, the collected representatives of the Spartan alliance, give their assent, and the Spartan plan for the restoration of Hippias is quickly abandoned.

Scholars have been puzzled by both the length and the anecdotal content of this speech. Is Sosicles trying to win his case by filibuster or by distracting his audience from the main point? Why didn't Herodotus allow him to make the kind of logical or theoretical argument against tyranny that he gives to Otanes in book 3, during the Persian debate over the three major forms of government (3.80)—a speech more in keeping with the tone of a high council session? Such questions, however, spring from a modern, literate way of thinking and are out of tune with an oral culture in which vivid storytelling trumps structured logic, even in debates over matters like foreign policy. In Sosicles' speech, tyranny ceases to be an abstract idea and is bodied forth in the saga of the Cypselid family, where it appears as something awesome and nightmarish, attended by supernatural omens and dreams, lurid appetites, and bizarre passions. The story holds the audience in its grip, arousing emotions of fear and horror that are certain to sway them toward Sosicles' position. A modern-day lawyer might use the same technique when attempting to sway a jury; law schools in fact now offer instruction in what they term narrative law, a style of argument based on the power of storytelling rather than on more legalistic, logical discourse.

Of course, Herodotus, as the chief storyteller of the *Histories,* stands in a relation to his audience different from that of a lawyer to a jury because he isn't trying to persuade us toward a particular course of action. Nevertheless, he too uses stories to reveal the true nature of events and the true character of people or even, in some cases, larger truths about the universe and the gods. His inset tales serve to define, in ways that mere exposition cannot, the world in which the main narrative takes place. Often one cannot say precisely what a given story means or link it to any single portion of that narrative; possibilities multiply and branch off in many directions, as we saw earlier in the case of Arion and the dolphin. One can sense, however, a coherent and complex intelligence behind these stories, such that when reading them we are learning to see the world as Herodotus sees it. For example, we begin to glimpse in the biology of lions and snakes, the subject of two by-now familiar "tales" in book 3, a mirror of the fall of kings and tyrants throughout the *Histories*. In other stories, such as those of Hermotimus, of Arion, and of Periander, we find other themes that resonate with the narrative as a whole: *tisis*, the redemption of innocence, and the victory of a certain kind of moral intelligence over its more brutish foes.

Readers can perhaps better appreciate the preliterate character of Herodotus's stories by comparing them with various remnants of oral culture still surviving in our print-saturated world. Gossip, for example, still entertains and delights us, especially when it allows us to get the "dirt" about the high and mighty—a boss or a professor, say. We have already seen that Herodotus shares this passion for behind-the-scenes glimpses of private, and in particular sexual, life, especially where rulers and lofty nobles are concerned. His desire to tell us what went on in the royal bedroom of Darius (3.134) and of Xerxes (9.108–13) shares in the impulses that motivate modern gossip: in such moments he brings kings and emperors closer to the human, all too human level of his audience and gives us a kind of covert power over the most mighty beings on earth. Similarly, the many tales told at the end of book 6 (chapters 123–31) about the wealthy Alcmaeonid family of Athens recall our modern-day absorption with the Kennedy clan, especially in the way they satisfy our curiosity about marital power plays at the highest level of society (see also 1.61). Yet Herodotus does not merely repeat the gossip of his contemporaries; ever the responsible narrator, he monitors it for fairness and accuracy. In book 6, for instance, he clears the Alcmaeonids of the cruelest charge rumor had leveled against them, the attempted betrayal of Athens after the battle of Marathon (chapter 124).

Personal reminiscences, especially war stories, are another area in which oral culture still thrives today, and Herodotus retells quite a few of these. In fact, when he narrates clashes be-

tween Greek and Persian armies or navies, vignettes of individual warriors, some of whom he clearly had interviewed in
person, predominate over the kind of general description one
finds in other military writers. Warfare, after all, is more compelling when seen through the lens of personal experience
than through maps and battle plans. Such orally transmitted
war stories, though mistrusted by many modern historians for
their inaccuracies and exaggerations, preserve a subjective
view of the past that even in the most literate of societies remains vital to a complete historical record. In the Japanese
cities of Hiroshima and Nagasaki, for example, the survivors
of the atomic bomb began to feel that history books alone
failed to capture their experience, and as a result a society of
storytellers known as *kataribe* has arisen in recent years to describe what happened when the bombs fell.

Other oral stories, often those we tell to our closest confidants or psychiatrists, describe family-centered psychic and
emotional experiences and serve as a vehicle for self-exploration. Many Herodotean stories similarly deal with familial
relationships and often follow universal patterns that overlap
closely with those of myth—except that their action is set in the
recent past rather than in the age of heroes. Periander's family
provides a good illustration, not so much in the saga related by
Sosicles as in a sequel told by Herodotus himself in book 3.
Long after the death of Melissa, news that she had been mur-
dered by Periander reaches the ears of their son Lycophron,
then seventeen years old. The boy stages a silent rebellion
against his father, refusing to speak to him, and after being driven out of the palace becomes a ragged beggar, a walking em-
barrassment to the dynasty. Periander despairs of the boy and
sends him into exile on Corcyra, but in his old age he longs to
have Lycophron back to carry on the family rule. Still repelled
by his father, Lycophron agrees to assume power in Corinth

only if Periander first removes himself to Corcyra; but the Corcyraeans, unwilling to play host to such a notorious tyrant, prevent the swap by having Lycophron killed (3.50–53). Whatever its factual, historical content, the story as Herodotus presents it reads like a myth, exploring the same themes as the Orestes myth it partly parallels: the anguish felt by children caught between maternal and paternal loyalties, and the need (unfulfilled, in Lycophron's case) for an adolescent boy to prove himself by taking his father's place.

Another of Herodotus's stories develops the same mythic theme of the rivalry between a ruler and his offspring, this time pitting the young boy not against his father but his grandfather. The tale of Cyrus's birth and accession to power, told in gripping detail in book 1 (chapters 107 through 130), bears obvious comparison to the Oedipus myth: in both cases a baby boy is exposed in the wilderness by its royal family, only to be discovered and raised by humble shepherds; having grown to manhood, the foundling seizes his rightful position on the throne by destroying his royal forebear. The same pattern, interestingly enough, can be seen in the Hebrew myth of Moses, though with the class structure reversed: the child of destiny is abandoned by humble parents and adopted by royal ones. The universality of such patterns shows that these stories, as they were passed from one teller to the next, were reshaped along the lines of elemental human experience: kings, queens, and princes became archetypal grandparents, parents, and children, and accounts of historical events gradually became vehicles for exploring primal fears, needs, and desires. To what degree Herodotus helped in reshaping these tales himself cannot be known, but plainly the mythic imagination of fifth-century Greece had been at work on them before they got written down in the *Histories*.

Still other Herodotean stories come not from the lofty realm of myth but from the folktale world, a place in which clever, rascally tricksters win out over the great and mighty; and here, too, Herodotus's materials can be recognized as belonging to oral tradition, especially that of the Near East. The tale of the nameless Egyptian thief who outsmarts the pharaoh Rhampsinitus (2.121), for instance, is a classic of the genre familiar to us from the medieval Arabic tales of Ali Baba. Another typical folktale hero is Perdiccas, the founder of the royal dynasty of Macedon, as described in book 8 (137–8). Perdiccas was the youngest of three brothers serving as poor laborers on the estate of a petty king. Whenever the queen baked bread for the three, Perdiccas's loaf grew to twice the size of the others, and the king, interpreting this as an omen of future greatness, threw all three of them out. When the brothers asked for their pay, the king pointed to a circle of sunlight on the floor beneath the palace chimney-hole, saying, "There are your wages for you." Clever Perdiccas spotted his opportunity and traced the outline of the sunlight with his knife, making a circle around the hearth—a ritual gesture by which, in ancient cultures, one takes possession of a house! This Perdiccas, the youngest brother blessed by fortune and the loyal servant who triumphs over his unjust master, has much in common with a Jewish folktale hero, Joseph of the Book of Genesis, as well as with his latter-day avatars.

In many places in the *Histories*, then, Herodotus has dipped into the great ocean of oral tales that washed all through the fifth-century Greek world, a world in which the use of writing was just beginning to become widespread. His work stands on the cusp of two eras, drawing heavily on the oral traditions of archaic Greece but recasting these in a way made possible by the new medium of the book. Transitions from orality to literacy are rare events in the history of culture because most societies go through them only once; it is an even rarer stroke of luck if an author of Herodotus's intelligence and grace happens to be on the scene when such a transition occurs. His *Histories* reflects the unique moment in which he lived, when writing had become advanced enough to capture the oral tradition, but not yet far enough advanced to kill it off.

Part of the artistry that makes storytellers great is the style in which their stories are told, and in this respect, too, Herodotus is among the greatest that we can read in any language. His style was widely celebrated for its charm, delight, and sweetness by ancient Greek and Roman men of letters; his clarity, simplicity, and vividness come through admirably in English translations, though of course many of his subtler effects—in particular, the musical lilt of his Ionic dialect—get lost. The overall character of Herodotus's style has been admirably summed up for the Greekless reader by Aubrey de Selincourt, who put the *Histories* into English for the Penguin edition: "Herodotus' prose has the flexibility, ease and grace of a man superbly talking." No other Greek prose author gives us this same sense of being *talked* to; Thucydides and Plato are clearly *writing*, even in passages in which they represent the speeches or conversations of their characters.

One feature of Herodotus's discursive style that *can* be felt even in English translation is his habit of marking off stories, anecdotes, and digressions with symmetrical "bookend" sentences: he first tells us what he's about to tell us, and then when he's done he tells us what he's told us. For example, in telling the story of Gyges and Candaules' wife, Herodotus begins (1.7), "The leadership that belonged to the Heraclids went over to the line of Croesus, known as the Mermnads, in the following way," and then concludes (1.14), "In that way, then, the

Mermnads obtained the tyranny, after taking it away from the Heraclids." One can see how such bookends help put readers (or listeners) on notice that they are departing from or returning to the main story line, but it is interesting to note that Herodotus uses them even when they serve no such purpose. Thus, in describing Cambyses' reconnaissance mission to the Ethiopians in book 3, Herodotus mentions that, among other things, the Persian king wanted to know whether the Table of the Sun really existed, and adds,

> The Table of the Sun is said to be something like the following: There is a meadow on the city outskirts filled with all variety of boiled meats, and on it those citizens who are in charge on each occasion place the meat, managing this at night, while during the day, anyone who wants comes and dines; but the natives say that the earth itself produces the food every time. So, the so-called Table of the Sun is said to be something like that. (3.18)

In this case the bookend sentences surround only a single sentence of text, so Herodotus need hardly have been concerned that his audience would lose his train of thought. But the use of such bookends is a pervasive feature of oral storytelling, as is clear from its frequency in Homer and other early poets; it serves Herodotus not only as a functional device but as a feature of style, a way to make the end of his stories come round to their starting point and to mark their completion. (A modern American storyteller, Garrison Keillor, uses a similar technique, opening each of his radio monologues with "It's been a quiet week in Lake Wobegon, my hometown" and closing with "That's the news from Lake Wobegon. . . .")

Herodotus's style reveals his closeness to the oral culture of archaic Greece in other ways as well. His sentences rarely use the kind of complex structures that would become com-

monplace only a few decades after his death; clauses are often
connected to each other by the simple "and," whereas a later
writer would prefer a relative pronoun or subordinating con-
junction. Some of his long, elaborate sentences start to get tan-
gled in the middle, so that Herodotus has to yank them forcibly
back onto the grammatical track; others crash along from one
point to the next with the author only barely hanging onto the
reins, as in this summary of the career of King Phraortes of the
Medes:

> Afterward, once he had gained control of these two tribes
> [the Medes and Persians] and held both of them secure, he
> began to subdue Asia, going from one tribe to another,
> until he mounted an attack on the Assyrians, and in par-
> ticular those Assyrians who used to hold Ninus and who
> formerly were rulers of all, but at *that* time stood alone,
> their allies having revolted, but in other respects were far-
> ing well in their own realm—mounting an attack on *them*,
> then, Phraortes himself was slain, after he had reigned for
> twenty-two years, and with him most of his army. (1.102)

One can imagine many different ways of arranging all this information artfully into a single sentence or of dividing it into
several sentences, but Herodotus seems to wade in at the beginning without a clear sense of where he is going to end up—
exactly as one does when one is speaking, not writing. Just as
the first European printed books, in the mid–fifteenth century,
sought to imitate the appearance of illuminated manuscripts,
so Herodotus the writer hews close to the style typical of the
oral tradition preceding him.

That is not to say, however, that Herodotus was a literary
child of nature who composed without technique or artistry.
When one looks closely one observes him using a variety of de-
vices to heighten the effect of his stories: foregrounding a word

borrowed from Homer at a moment of high drama or solemnity, for example, or causing his royal characters to speak in the stately, archaic diction of Athenian tragedy. But one does need to look closely to observe such touches; they are applied with a light hand and do not call attention to themselves. Rather, his most memorable sentences are those characterized by understatement, simplicity, and utter lack of self-consciousness, as in the opening sentences of two book 1 stories:

> This Candaules fell passionately in love with his own wife, and in his passion he considered her the most beautiful by far of all women. (1.8)

> Croesus had two children, of whom one was marred from birth—for he was a mute—but the other was by far the foremost of his peers; and his name was Atys. (1.34)

In such sentences one feels, just as one does in the Hebrew Bible, the candor and directness with which stories are told in an oral culture. It is the tale itself, the anticipation that something extraordinary is going to happen, that compels us to pull up our chairs and listen. The artistry of the narrator consists largely of simply allowing this magic to work.

IX REASON, CREDULITY, AND FAITH

THE SENSE OF A SPEAKING VOICE IN THE *HISTORIES,* OF SOMEONE "superbly talking," derives not only from its oral style but from the persona its narrator adopts and the way he addresses his audience. Herodotus somehow makes his readers into confidants; we are invited to share his ideas and interests, to think his thoughts, to see the world as he sees it. "He *tells* us things," as one writer has observed, the way a fond grandparent tells things to a wide-eyed child; one feels, more perceptibly than with most other authors ancient or modern, that he wants us to learn what he has learned. One can practically see him rubbing his hands together with delight when he is about to relate something really interesting, like the Egyptians' system for providing drinking water in an otherwise uncrossable Syrian desert:

> I'm going to tell something that few of those who make trading voyages to Egypt have observed: Even though ceramic ware is imported into Egypt every year, filled with wine, from all of Greece and in addition from Phoenicia, there is not a single empty wine jar, so to speak, anywhere to be seen. "Well, then how are these used up?" someone might ask. I'll tell this as well. Each village chief [in Egypt] must collect all the ware from his own town and bring it to Memphis; then others convey it from Memphis to this same Syrian desert, after filling it with water. (3.6)

Here Herodotus enters into a dialogue with his imagined audience, posing them an intellectual puzzle and then delivering
the punch line as though answering their eager entreaty. Although he never addresses his readers (or listeners) directly, he
gives the distinct impression throughout the *Histories,* in the
way he conveys information and explains his procedures, that
he knows they are present.

Herodotus becomes particularly animated when dealing
with puzzles, riddles, and logical problems, like the seeming
disappearance of the ceramic ware used in the Egyptian recy-
cling program. Almost invariably he shares his reasoning with
us as he attempts to resolve such problems, "taking us through
it" as one might say. When he performs arithmetic calculations,
as, for example, when he tallies up the numbers in Xerxes'
army and navy (7.184–86), he does his math out loud, as it
were, rather than merely presenting us with a total. (In some
cases this has permitted modern researchers to trace his mathematical errors; evidently Herodotus was skilled at addition
and multiplication but, like many of us, had some trouble with
long division.) With scientific problems he is equally candid,
often sharing with us four or five separate pieces of evidence
supporting his own hypothesis. Near the beginning of book 2,
for example, Herodotus examines the idea that the land of
Egypt originated as "the gift of the river," that is, as silt de-
posited by the river Nile. By extending this notion over a vast
length of time, he reasons that the place where Egypt now
stands must once have been a vast gulf, and then goes on to
mount a series of geological arguments:

> I have seen that Egypt juts forth from the surrounding land,
> and I have seen seashells uncovered in the mountains, and
> salt blossoming forth on the ground such that even the
> pyramids get eroded . . . and I have seen that Egypt is not

at all like the part of Arabia that borders it, nor of Libya . . .
but has black and friable soil, inasmuch as it was once
mud, a deposit carried down from Ethiopia by the river.
(2.12)

This is followed by a further, more convoluted point involving
the gradual elevation of the banks of the Nile (2.13). Clearly
Herodotus feels he must *convince* us, as though we were peers
at a modern-day scientific conference, rather than merely proclaim his opinions ex cathedra.

What is remarkable about such open discussions is not
only the intimacy they create between narrator and audience,
but the skill Herodotus displays in his analysis of scientific
problems. A bit further on in his discussion of the Nile, Herodotus gives perhaps his most virtuosic display of his deductive
powers. In a rather dense passage, chapters 20 through 27 of
book 2, Herodotus discusses the cause of the annual flooding
of the Nile—an event that mysteriously took place in summer,
the season when all other rivers were at lowest ebb—and dis-
misses three theories advanced by his contemporaries, men
whom he refers to rather scornfully as "some Greeks who wish
to become notable for their wisdom" (2.20). According to one
such thinker, the summer winds that blow south from the
Mediterranean push back the Nile's waters and cause them to
overflow; but, as Herodotus correctly points out, these winds
would affect other north-flowing rivers similarly, whereas no
river but the Nile floods in summer. A second thinker (probably Hecataeus) theorizes that the Nile has its source in the river
Ocean, the mythical and therefore magical body of water that
could presumably cause supernormal effects. Herodotus objects, based on the empirical standard of evidence I noted in
chapter VI, that no one has seen the river Ocean, and therefore
any theory based on it lies beyond the reach of investigation.

The third theory, however, Herodotus treats with the most gravity: the Nile's waters increase in summer because they are fed by melting snows at the river's origin (correct, as we now know). Against this "seemingly most reasonable" theory, Herodotus mounts a barrage of counterevidence:

> How, I ask, could the river flow out of snow—since it flows out of a hotter region, toward places that are generally cooler? For anyone who is able to think rationally about such things, the first and greatest proof that it is not reasonable for it to flow out of snow is furnished by the winds, since they blow hot out of those regions [where the river rises]. Second, the fact that this country is cloudless and never freezes; but it is always necessary that rain come within five days after a snowfall, so that, if there *were* any snow, this region would also have rain. Third, the people there are black on account of the heat; and, hawks and swallows stay there year round without leaving, whereas cranes, which flee the cold when it sets in in Scythian country, go to winter in these regions. If, then, it snowed even a little in the country through which the Nile flows and from which it rises, none of these things would be, as necessity demonstrates. (2.22)

A modern-day earth scientist might feel tempted to stand up and cheer, seeing Herodotus make such cogent inferences from a diverse body of evidence (even though several of the presuppositions on which his refutation is based are now known, like his conclusion, to be wrong).

But Herodotus truly astounds us when he goes on to offer his own theory to supersede the three he has just dismissed. He suggests, ingeniously, that during the winter, the sun gets blown to the south by storm winds—a standard explanation in his day for the observed precession of the equinoxes—and

causes the Nile to lose more of its water than usual to evapo-
ration; in summer, when the sun moves northward again, it
draws from all rivers equally and the Nile therefore *appears* to
flood when it returns to normal strength. He then tests this
model of summer Nile floods by using it to explain why rivers
in Greece flood in *winter:* Nile water drawn up by the winter
sun gets blown northward, according to known wind patterns,
and falls as rain on the other side of the Mediterranean. Then,
as a final stage in the testing of his theory, Herodotus performs
a thought experiment to determine, as any good scientist would,
its universality. He imagines the climates of North and South
reversed, with the sun moving northward over Europe in winter instead of southward over Africa, and hypothesizes that
under those conditions the Ister (or Danube) would flood in
summer just like the Nile (2.26). None of this can be demonstrated in a laboratory, of course, but it shows Herodotus
thinking about how his Nile hypothesis fits into the larger pattern of global symmetry that makes the northern and southern
halves of the globe mirror one another.

Such feats of problem solving and scientific reasoning are
counterbalanced, however, by passages in the *Histories* in which
Herodotus shows himself capable of sloppy thinking and
chopped logic. Consider, for example, his treatment of a popular story concerning how Croesus and his army crossed the
river Halys when they attacked Persia (1.75). Herodotus says
that Croesus used existing bridges that spanned the Halys,
even though "the prevailing report of the Greeks" offered a
different account: the Greek sage Thales, who had accompanied the expedition, altered the river's course, causing half or
(according to an alternate version) all of its waters to flow behind the advancing army. "But I do not believe this story," Herodotus proclaims, "for how would they have crossed the river
again when making their way back?" Perspicuous readers will

feel somewhat befuddled by the reasoning Herodotus applies to this problem, for why couldn't Thales perform the same trick twice—or even leave the Halys divided into fordable halves, so as to spare the trouble of altering its course again on the return journey?

Perhaps Herodotus's thinking about the story of Thales and the Halys river was skewed by his presuppositions about its reliability; for Thales was a legendary figure about whom many fabulous tales were told (he has been compared to the Merlin figure of Arthurian myth). In other words, where Herodotus applies his mind to a report he has heard, rather than to observations he has made, a new set of considerations enters his thought process: where did the story originate, and how trustworthy is its source? The Thales story seems to be too widely diffused for a successful trace, but in his handling of other such reports—by far the most common intellectual problem he confronts in the *Histories*—Herodotus plays the role not just of logician but of police detective or newspaper reporter, following a trail of information back to its point of origin. In these cases, too, he likes to conduct his investigation openly, with full disclosure of results, as though enjoying the thrill of the chase and anticipating that we, his audience, will share in that thrill.

Herodotus takes us along on two particularly knotty investigations in books 2 and 4, where he deals with information about the southernmost and northernmost edges of the earth. In both of these, as in the rejections of the river Ocean we looked at earlier, he draws firm distinctions between empirical and hearsay evidence, noting that he himself has seen, for example, the upper Nile as far as the city of Elephantine but learned only from hearsay what lay beyond that point (2.29). Even when he relies on evidence supplied by someone else, he notifies us how far *that* person's knowledge extends, as with the information about northern Europe supplied by the poet Aristeas: "Concerning the land about which my account has begun to be told, no one knows with certainty what lies north of it; for I've been unable to inquire of anyone who claimed to be an eyewitness. And not even Aristeas . . . claims in his poem to have journeyed farther than the Issedones, but described what lies north of there from hearsay, claiming the Issedones as his informants. But as far as we are able to go with certainty by means of hearsay, up to the outer limit, will all be presented here" (4.16). In passages like this Herodotus establishes a kind of information map with concentric zones of reliability: data based on what Aristeas *saw* comes to Herodotus at one remove, whereas what he *heard* comes at two removes and is proportionally less trustworthy. In his most far-reaching investigation, his inquiry into the course of the upper Nile in book 2, Herodotus penetrates to the fifth such zone, tracing a single report through four previous stages of transmission—some Greeks from Cyrene had told Herodotus a story that they heard from King Etearchus of the Ammonians, who heard it from some visiting Nasamonians, who in turn heard it from a group of their own countrymen—to the effect that the Nile arose in a great marshland lying west of the Sahara desert and inhabited by dwarfish black men (2.32). Herodotus passes no judgment of his own on the truth of the story but reminds us, as he reaches its end, that he only repeats what the Cyrenaeans have told him.

By providing such a scrupulous account of his story's sources, he signals his audience that they are entitled to form their own conclusions about its content. In other cases, however, Herodotus himself acts as arbiter of a story's veracity, presenting it to his audience in order to show why it should not be believed. Indeed, it is a vexing, perhaps impossible task to find a consistent methodology or uniform standard of evidence in Herodotus's many examinations of second- and third-

hand reports. Some he rejects only because they contain a logical flaw or inconsistency; thus the mythical river Eridanos,
supposed by the Greek poets to flow through western Europe,
is unmasked by way of an ingenious linguistic argument:

> For my part I don't accept that there is a river, called Eri-
> danos by the barbarians, that flows into the northern sea.
> . . . The very name Eridanos indicts the story, since it is a
> Greek name, not barbarian, and hence made up by some
> poet or other. (3.115)

In other cases, however, such as that of the river Ocean, Herodotus rejects geographic reports simply because he lacks
eyewitness confirmation. In still other cases, Herodotus tries to
save an implausible story by rationalizing or reinterpreting it.
Faced with a Scythian report that the far north of Europe cannot be traveled because the air is filled with feathers, he infers
that "the Scythians and their neighbors speak of *feathers* as a
figure for *snow*" (4.31). A keen critical mind is at work on all
these dilemmas, but it does not operate by consistent or uniform principles and indeed exhibits some rather surprising
lapses on occasion. In some of his more fabulous accounts, like
the tale of the giant gold-gathering ants who inhabit the
deserts of India (3.102–5), Herodotus raises no red flags what-
soever but seems to abandon himself to the sheer pleasure of
the story and to expect his audience to do the same.

Surprisingly, Herodotus is often at his most credulous
when reporting on investigations he himself has made in foreign lands. In Egypt, for example, he quite willingly swallows
some of the more improbable tall tales he hears from native
guides. On being shown the differing thicknesses of Persian
and Egyptian skulls, for instance, he accepts the local hypothesis that shaved Egyptian heads grow thicker skulls as a result
of exposure to the sun (3.12). At the Great Pyramid of Cheops,

he trusts his guide's report that a hieroglyphic inscription recorded the amount spent on onions, garlic, and radishes to feed the construction crew (2.125). Most notoriously, on seeing some as yet unidentified heap of fossils or bones in the mountains of Arabia, he believes, apparently again on local authority, that he stands before the remains of flying snakes (2.75). From our modern-day, scientific perspective, Herodotus the traveler can seem a wide-eyed or naive tourist or, as one scholar rather ungenerously termed him, "the happy idiot of Greek historiography." But we must keep in mind that Herodotus was one of only a few Greeks to have visited these far-off places, and perhaps the first to have gone there as an explorer rather than a merchant or mercenary. He bore with him a vast array of preconceptions about the wonders they held, and these inevitably made him readier to believe what he was told or even to see things as he thought they should appear. The first explorers of the New World, who returned to Europe with reports of gold, precious stones, and semihuman monstrosities, showed considerably less faithfulness to empirical reality than did Herodotus; and many a modern traveler to Egypt has returned devoutly convinced of the supernatural phenomena described by local guides.

Whatever logical tools he brought to bear on scientific problems and geographic reports, Herodotus faced a much different set of issues when he dealt with divine apparitions and miracles, as he does in so many tales in the *Histories*. Though the credibility of such supernatural phenomena to some degree relies upon that of their sources, Herodotus's own religious attitudes and beliefs, his sense of how the divine operates in the world, play a much bigger role in determining how he handles these stories. Furthermore, because those attitudes were subject to powerful social sanctions, we cannot properly assess

Herodotus's statements on religious topics except against the background of the times in which he wrote.

The second half of the fifth century was a period of intense religious controversy and even crisis in the Greek world and especially in the city of Athens. Traditional beliefs came increasingly into question as the natural sciences, spawned in Ionia but now rapidly spreading through the Greek mainland, advanced. At times, the tension between an understanding of the world based on scientific principles and one based on traditional ideas about the gods erupted into open hostility or cultural warfare, and some of the more progressive Greek scientific thinkers found themselves in peril. For example, the philosopher Anaxagoras, a close contemporary of Herodotus, was indicted by the Athenians for impiety after he dared to explain certain aspects of nature without reference to the gods; and although the case of Socrates is more complex, he too fell victim, in part, to the religious conservatism of his age. When scientific inquiry came into conflict with religious tradition, most fifth-century Greeks chose to defend the faith; to do otherwise could pose a serious challenge to public morality, just as it could, say, in Europe of the Renaissance, and as it still does in some quarters today.

Inasmuch as he considered his work a *historiē*, or inquiry, using logical and scientific approaches to investigate the past, Herodotus risked offending the religious values still held by the majority in his culture. Yet he was careful to reduce the tension his work might have caused and to avoid choosing sides in the contest between science and faith. His way of explaining the origin of a gorge in the mountains of Thessaly, for example, shows him neatly tiptoeing around a potential trouble spot:

> The Thessalians themselves say that Poseidon made the gorge through which the river Peneus flows, and their ac-

count is reasonable; for whoever supposes that Poseidon causes earthquakes, and that clefts in the earth caused by earthquakes are the work of this god, would say, if he saw this one, that Poseidon made it; for this cleft in the mountains *is* the result of an earthquake, as it seems to me. (7.129)

Just as a seasoned diplomat uses vague language to reconcile opposing factions, Herodotus here skirts the crucial question of whether Poseidon really does cause earthquakes, a question he certainly could not have answered without alienating segments of his audience. On another occasion, Herodotus directly refutes a mythic tale about Heracles on the grounds that it couldn't possibly have happened the way the Greeks report—but then, with what may well be sincere trepidation, he asks, "May the gods and heroes be kindly to me, now that I have spoken these things" (2.45). Though the story he rejects concerns something Heracles did while still a mortal and thus poses no direct challenge to the gods per se, Herodotus nevertheless shrinks from crossing a gulf that might separate him from the traditions enshrined in ancient myth.

A modern reader may wrongly suppose that Herodotus speaks only figuratively or ironically when he asks that the gods forgive him for questioning tradition. Our age is accustomed to regard God as a transcendent being, involved in earthly affairs only indirectly and in abstract or imperceptible ways. Herodotus, however, makes no such presumption and reports a wide variety of miracles in the *Histories* without casting any doubt on their divine origin. Granted, he is not prepared to believe that the Olympian gods appear openly and intervene in human affairs, as they do in Homer; thus he chastises his countrymen for believing a hoax contrived by Pisistratus, tyrant of Athens, involving a tall, beautiful woman dressed up to look like Athena (1.60). But he seems entirely unfazed by stories of nameless divinities, often distinguished by their extraordinary size or beauty, who appear in the midst of battles (6.117, 8.38, 8.84) or who speak to human beings in dreams (7.12), exactly as Homer's gods do (these superhuman figures should probably be regarded as heroes rather than gods, that is, as beings who were once mortal but achieved divine status at their deaths and who occupy a kind of middle zone between earth and heaven). Herodotus does not shrink either from recording that minor deities, like the goat-footed Pan (6.105) and the divinized Helen of Sparta (6.61), had made appearances in Greece as recently as the preceding century. There can be no doubt of Herodotus's earnestness when he retells such stories, and no suspicion that he laughs up his sleeve at those who had reported them. Though he might scoff at the idea that Athena herself had come to Athens to restore Pisistratus or that sixth-century Athenians might believe such a thing, he does not gainsay the grandchildren of those Athenians when they build a shrine of Pan based on what they claim the god himself had told them to do.

On a few occasions in the *Histories* Herodotus loudly proclaims his allegiance to the traditional piety that saw the gods and heroes as directly involved in human affairs. In book 8, for example, he describes how a Persian contingent besieging the coastal city of Potidaea was wiped out by a sudden, anomalous inrush of tide. He then remarks,

> The Potidaeans say that the cause of this tidal wave and of the Persian disaster was this: Those Persians who were destroyed by the sea had treated impiously a shrine of Poseidon and a statue of the god standing outside the city walls. And in stating this cause they seem to me to speak rightly. (8.129)

The idea that the gods take direct vengeance on those who dishonor their temples would have seemed antiquated or naive to some of Herodotus's contemporaries, as no doubt it does to most modern readers. Yet Herodotus seems proud to embrace it, as he does again in a later passage (9.65) explaining why the Persians who were killed at Plataea had been unable to find refuge in a grove of Demeter, the goddess whose temple in Attica they had earlier burned. The story of the miraculous salvation of the Delphic oracle from a Persian invasion force (8.35–39), a tale presumably invented by the Delphic priests but retold by Herodotus in a style breathless with amazement, conveys the same impression: our author takes his stand with the believers at a time when, in parts of the Greek world at least, that stratum of society was increasingly on the defensive. One finds no traces in the *Histories* of the scoffing sophistication of Aristophanes' Socrates—so much more in tune with our own, postmodern sensibilities—who, only a few years after the likely death of Herodotus, would point out in the play *The Clouds* that the gods, far from defending their shrines from attack or defilement, often destroy them themselves with earthquakes and bolts of lightning.

Much the same can be said regarding Herodotus's treatment of lesser divine phenomena like dreams, portents, and oracles. Although he acknowledges on two occasions that the priestess who delivered the oracles at Delphi could be bribed (5.63, 6.66), he mostly ignores the possibility, deemed a certainty by modern historians, that the profit motive largely dictated the responses of this most mercantile of Greek shrines. Similarly, he believes strongly in the efficacy of seers and prophets, despite his awareness that prophecies could be counterfeited for political motives (7.6). He trusts in particular the oracular verses of one Bakis, whom he quotes on several occasions in books 8 and 9 and whose predictions he defends in highly polemical language:

> I cannot refute oracles by saying that they are not true, not being willing to try to reject those that speak unambiguously. . . . When Bakis speaks without ambiguity, I do not dare to utter counterarguments about oracles, nor will I accept them from others. (8.77)

The vehemence of Herodotus's tone here indicates he is responding to particular critics of Bakis or of prophecy verses in general, and indeed, he may have added all the Bakis quotations to his work at a late stage in order to underscore his point (the lack of connection between these passages and their immediate context suggests they were pasted in after books 8 and 9 were already written, and in fact some scholars believe that someone other than Herodotus may have added them). If these passages date from the later years of Herodotus's life, we can well imagine the kind of debate that gave rise to them: for it was about this time, the opening years of the Peloponnesian War, that disputes over prophecy were at their hottest in Athens. The following passage of Thucydides' account of the great plague that struck Athens in 430, for example, makes a pointed contrast to Herodotus's pious declaration of faith:

> In this calamity, as is natural, people recalled the following verse, said by the older generation to have been uttered long before: "A Dorian war will come, and a plague [*loimos*] along with it." But a controversy arose among the populace as to whether the verse of the ancient poets had named a plague [*loimos*] or a famine [*limos*]; and as one would expect in the present circumstance, the view that "plague" had been written won out, for people were fashioning their recollection according to what they were experiencing. I

suppose that if another Dorian war comes upon them and after that a *famine* happens to take place, they will recite the verse *that* way, as would be natural. (2.54)

The various passages cited above show that Herodotus must be counted among the more conservative members of a society that included a wide spectrum of religious attitudes; but in no case does he express the kind of reactionary anger that led to the indictment of Anaxagoras and helped condemn Socrates to death, and that is often voiced, in caricature anyway, by crusty, aged Athenians in the comedies of Aristophanes. Though he tends to side with traditional piety in religious matters, Herodotus remains open to the new thinking and does not feel the need (as did some of his younger contemporaries) to push conflicts between the two toward a showdown. A good example of his open-mindedness comes in book 7, when Xerxes and his uncle Artabanus debate the origin of a dream that has commanded Xerxes to mount an invasion of Greece. Xerxes asserts the view that Herodotus himself subscribes to throughout the *Histories*, namely, that dreams are sent by the gods as warnings or prophecies of the future, though he also admits to some uncertainty on this score (7.15). Artabanus, for his part, presents what we would now regard as a psychological explanation of dreams:

> These things are not divine, my child; rather, the dreams that visit humankind in their wanderings are such as I shall teach you, being older than you by many years. The visions that most often visit in dreams are the things that the dreamer thinks about during the day; in our case, we were very much involved with this invasion during the days before this. (7.16)

Artabanus, too, concedes the possibility that his view may be mistaken, and so the two men agree to the experiment of having Artabanus sleep in Xerxes' bed to see if the same dream will visit *him*. The test, as we could certainly have predicted, supports Xerxes' traditional point of view; but the outcome is perhaps less telling than either the discussion that precedes it, in which Herodotus allows both views to be persuasively argued, or the decision to submit the issue to a trial.

The scientific experiment performed by Xerxes and Artabanus to test the divine origin of dreams recalls Herodotus's own logical tests of the theories explaining the Nile floods and reminds us of other, similar experiments described at various points in the *Histories* (for example, Darius's comparison of Greek and Indian rites of the dead, discussed in chapter VII above). As a rational thinker and a practitioner of *historiē*, Herodotus is fascinated by all such experiments and pursues them himself with a tenacity worthy of an Enlightenment philosophe. But as a pious adherent of his society's more conservative religious views, he preferred to leave the gods and heroes beyond the reach of such inquiry and to accept that miracles really did happen only a few decades before his time. Thus one senses little in his work of the growing tension between reason and faith in late-fifth-century Athens; a man of exceptionally broad spirit, he managed to contain both within the vast amplitude of the *Histories*. In the end, his keen critical and rational impulses are counterbalanced by his belief that, as he tells us himself, "anything can happen, in the fullness of time" (5.9).

X THE FIFTH CENTURY: WARS BETWEEN WORLDS

ALMOST FIFTY YEARS AFTER THE FALL OF CROESUS'S LYDIAN EM-pire to the Persians, the city of Sardis was captured again, this time by the Greeks. The cities of Ionia, having lived under the Persians during all that half century, began a revolt against their masters in 499 B.C.; as a first strike, they sent an army eastward from Miletus and took Sardis, the Persian regional capital nearest their own territory. Accompanying the Ionian rebels were troops from Athens and Eretria, the two states of European Greece that had elected to aid them (Sparta, the reigning superpower of the Hellenic world, had declined to participate). After burning the city, the combined force marched back to the coast, where a Persian army caught up to it and soundly defeated it. At this point the Athenian contingent, consisting of twenty ships carrying about two hundred men each, detached itself and returned to Athens, its support of the rebellion at an end. During their few days of participation, however, these ships had become, as Herodotus says in a portentous phrase adapted from Homer's *Iliad,* "the beginning of evils for both the Greeks and barbarians"—for King Darius could not permit such European disruption of his frontier and became committed, as Herodotus tells it, to retribution against Athens and ultimately to the conquest of Greece.

Herodotus begins his account of the Ionian rebellion at chapter 28 of book 5, and this chapter might be called the opening of the second half of the *Histories:* The "world tour" conducted in the first half has been completed, and from this point on the narrative will focus almost exclusively on the conflict between Greeks and Persians. As if to mark the boundary between the two halves, Herodotus creates a structural parallel between the first phase of the Ionian revolt in book 5 and the first phase of Croesus's war against Cyrus in book 1. Before undertaking to fight the Persians, in book 1, Croesus had sent messengers to Sparta and Athens seeking alliance, and Herodotus had seized on those embassies as opportunities to describe the internal conditions of both leading Greek cities (1.56–70). Then in book 5, Aristagoras of Miletus, the leader of the Ionian revolt, journeys to both Sparta and Athens seeking alliance in *his* war against the Persians, and Herodotus again stops to examine both cities (5.38–97). In this way he introduces, then revisits, the two main actors in his historical drama—the two states that will, in the final act, lead the defense of the Greek mainland.

Because the events in the second half of the *Histories* are more circumscribed, in terms of both time and space, than those of the first and because Herodotus interrupts them far less frequently with flashbacks and digressions, I need not outline them here in any depth. It would be otiose, moreover, to summarize the events Herodotus himself narrates in such gripping detail; the story is much better told by him than by any of his successors, which is why so many Greek history instructors assign the *Histories* rather than textbook accounts of the Persian Wars. Nevertheless, a few remarks regarding the broad significance of these events may be useful to those encountering them for the first time. I should stress once again that I do not wish to reduce the *Histories* to a mere record of historical facts or to critique Herodotus on the basis of whether he got things wrong or right; I seek rather to highlight some of the larger themes in the period he describes, a period in which

European Greece met the greatest peril it had ever faced and, miraculously, triumphed.

At the opening of the fifth century the Persians had absorbed three-quarters of the ancient world into their empire and seemed poised to snap up the remaining quarter. Darius had established a beachhead in Europe by his conquest of Thrace, quite possibly intending from the start to add mainland Greece to his already extensive and profitable Hellenic territories in Asia Minor. However that may be, the involvement of Athens and Eretria in the Ionian revolt of 499 gave the Persians both a pretext and a pressing imperative to undertake the conquest of Greece. The aid sent to the rebels by these two cities, though slight and, on the Athenian side, short-lived, had nonetheless demonstrated that the national and racial ties that bound the Greeks together were stronger than the divide between the continents. Darius now knew that his western frontier would never be secure so long as Europe remained unsubdued; although he no doubt longed to punish Athens and Eretria for their participation in the burning of Sardis, as Herodotus claims, his larger objective from the start, as Herodotus is also aware (6.44), was to swallow Greece whole.

Probably the Persians imagined they would not have to fight for control of Greece so much as frighten it into submission; they held an immense advantage in numbers of men, in ships (once the Phoenician navy had been lured into their service), and in financial resources. Darius sent heralds to all the cities of Greece in advance of the invasion of 490, demanding the tokens of submission to Persia, gifts of earth and water; and according to Herodotus many gave these, prompted in part by the oracle at Delphi, whose priests had either been suborned by Persia or genuinely saw no point in resisting. Athens and Sparta, however, answered Darius by killing the heralds who visited them, a story narrated by Herodotus in a flashback

(7.133): The Athenians threw the messengers into a pit and the Spartans into a well, thus giving them their earth and water. Neither city seems to have known what the other was doing, but the fact that their actions turned out to be complementary underscores the significance of this historical moment. Out of their separate decisions to defy Darius's dictates, a remarkable alliance between the two states, so different in every way except for their shared commitment to the autonomy of Greece, was born. The progress of this alliance through the numerous crises that threatened to sunder it forms one of the central and most memorable themes of the second half of the *Histories*. Throughout the next twelve years, Athens and Sparta would continue to complement one another in a way that neatly reverses their use of earth and water to defy Darius's heralds— Sparta contributing her highly trained land army to the united defense of Greece, Athens her newly acquired fleet of warships and skilled crewmen.

Before becoming a sea power, however (see 7.144), Athens was compelled to face its first test on land and, what was more terrifying, without the aid of Sparta. When Darius's seaborne invasion force, led by Datis and Artaphrenes, landed at Marathon in the spring of 490, only twenty-four miles north of the city walls, Athens hastily petitioned Sparta for aid, but the Spartans, invoking a religious prohibition they would return to several times in the coming years, claimed to be unable to march during a festival they were then holding (6.106). Thus the Athenians stood virtually alone at Marathon, aided only by a handful of neighboring Plataeans; Athens was forced to use its hoplite army—never one of the impressive land forces in the Greek world—against an enemy who outnumbered it perhaps two to one. How did these largely untested troops find the courage to charge such a formidable invader, hurling themselves, as Herodotus reminds us, at foreigners whose dress and

armor they had never before glimpsed? The answer is not entirely clear, partly owing to Herodotus's vague description of
the battle (6.108–17); certainly the courage and initiative of the
Athenian leader Miltiades was a decisive factor. But we should
also bear in mind that, in all the land battles the Greeks fought
against Asians, they faced men who were vastly less well
trained and organized than themselves and who were outfitted
with leather clothing and wicker shields rather than with
heavy bronze armor. Better equipment and better tactics enabled few to defeat many, as they have often done since. The
vase paintings and sculptural friezes in which the Greeks depicted their wars against the Persians clearly reveal this mis-
match of weaponry: Greek hoplites carrying metal shields and
long thrusting spears and protected by helmet and breastplate
attack leather-suited barbarians wielding short daggers and fitting arrows to bows. Add to this imbalance the vastly better cohesion of the Greek phalanx as compared with the swarming
Asian cohorts, united under Persian command but fighting in
diverse indigenous styles and speaking a welter of languages,
and one can easily understand the courage that inspired the
charge at Marathon as well as the hugely lopsided (and no
doubt exaggerated) casualty figures Herodotus gives for all
such infantry battles.

The Athenian victory at Marathon was nonetheless accounted a miracle by the Hellenic world, and it gave new
courage to the Greeks when, in 480, Darius's son Xerxes
mounted a much larger and more determined invasion of their
homeland. Herodotus fast-forwards to this new episode at the
opening of book 7 by covering the nine intervening years in
only a few paragraphs, but once he has reached it he slows the
narrative of the *Histories* to its most measured pace yet, following events week by week and even day by day. The last
three books of the *Histories* cover only about a year of histori-

cal time, as compared with the decade that passes in the two preceding books and quarter century in the two before that; as for books 1 and 2, one could say that their time span is somewhere between seventeen thousand years and thirty, depending on what event one chooses as the start of the historical clock. Thus, although the narrative's tempo varies within any one book so as to give fuller treatment to important events, it also slows by steady increments as it moves forward from 560 to 479—one of Herodotus's more unique and original choices for the grand plan of his *Histories*. Similarly, in terms of geographic scope, Herodotus gradually zooms in from the vast panorama of book 1 to tight close-ups on central Greece and the western Aegean in 7 through 9. Because the events described in these last three books eclipse what precedes them in magnitude and import, Herodotus structures the books themselves as the narrative crescendo of the entire work.

In his preparations for attack, Xerxes abandoned his father's pretense of aiming only at the punishment of Athens; the size of the new expedition proclaimed that it was designed to subdue all of Greece. As a result, the Greeks now undertook a more serious effort at joint defense, meeting twice, in 481 and 480, in a Panhellenic congress at the isthmus of Corinth (7.145–46, 172–75). The convening of a council of allied cities may seem to us an unremarkable event, accustomed as we are to international diplomacy and to colloquies even of bitterest rivals; but in the Greek world, such a thing had never happened, that anyone knew of, since the Trojan War. Only under extreme pressure from a common foe were the contentious cities of the Greek world able to put aside their differences and follow a common leader, Sparta. Even proud Athens, as Herodotus relates much further on in his narrative (8.3), agreed to Spartan leadership not only of land forces, but also of the navy, even though Athens had contributed most of the ships. "The Athenians considered it essential that Greece survive and believed that if there was a dispute about the [naval] leadership, Greece would perish; and they considered aright," Herodotus comments, and then, perhaps quoting from some lost poem, observes, "Internal division [*stasis emphulos*] is as much worse than like-minded warfare as war is worse than peace" (8.3). Never before could the phrase *stasis emphulos*, used by Solon in the early sixth century to refer to civil war within a single *polis*, have described a conflict *between* city-states. The ideal of a Panhellenic unity had been born, but as we shall see in the final chapter of this volume it was fated to have a short, though glorious, life.

Not only in his discussion of the leadership issue, but in one other important passage, Herodotus credits Athens more than Sparta with having fostered and preserved the unity of the Greek forces. In his most famous and perhaps most astute piece of tactical analysis, he asserts that the Athenian fleet had been vital to the Greeks' victory over Xerxes because the Persians had to be beaten on both land and sea if they were to be stopped (7.139). Left to themselves, the Spartans, who were no sailors, might have opted to defend only the Peloponnese, a peninsula that could be easily walled off at its isthmus and defended with a small number of hoplites. But the Persians, in the absence of the Athenian navy to stop them, could simply have sailed around any such wall and landed troops wherever they pleased. Thus, although the Spartans were nominally the leaders of the allied Greek defense force, the Athenians held the key to its success. This harmonious imbalance of strengths would produce some tense and nearly fatal conflicts within the alliance but would also ensure that, in the end, it held together.

United in arms, the two leading cities of Greece also became united in suffering, as Herodotus relates in books 7 and 8 of the *Histories*. The tragic Greek defeat at the pass of Thermopylae in book 7 fell most heavily upon the Spartans, who

lost one of their kings and a contingent of three hundred hoplites when the troops guarding the pass found themselves
outflanked and trapped. A short while later, Athens had to endure the sack of its city and the destruction of its temples,
though Themistocles had wisely evacuated most of the population and movable goods while there was still time. The two
leading allies shared equally in the nobility that comes of surviving adversity, and they also shared in the glories of victory:
of the two large battles that decided the war in Greece, Salamis
and Plataea, Herodotus credits Themistocles and Athens with
success in the former, and (though less decisively) Pausanias
and the Spartans in the latter. Had the two cities been more
alike in their social and political makeup, their combined effort
against the Persians might have cemented a long and warm alliance, just as, for example, the United States and Britain have
been more closely bound by their collaborations in two world
wars. Instead, like the United States and Soviet Russia, the two
former allies soon grew mistrustful of one another as they vied
for dominance in the postwar world. But in those develop-
ments lay the seeds of another war and, as far as Herodotus
was concerned anyway, another story.

In the last battle described in the *Histories*, the Greek assault on the Persian naval station at Mycale—a battle concurrent
with Plataea but, again perforce, narrated consecutively—the
great circle that had begun twenty years earlier with Aristagoras's mission to Athens and Sparta was finally closed. The
European Greeks succeeded at last in liberating their Asian
kinsmen from the Persians, and the Greek cities of Anatolia
threw off the yoke they had borne since the time of Croesus.
Persian power, which had been growing and expanding ever
since Cyrus established the empire, began at last to retract.
Never again would the Persian state reach the size and mag-
nificence it attained under Darius, and never again would a

Persian army or navy threaten the Greeks in Europe. Indeed, future battles would be fought on Persian territory, as both the Athenians and Spartans took the offensive in Asia, intermittently, throughout most of the next century.

The course of world history is filled with fateful might-have-beens, but the Greek defeat of the Persian invasions of Europe is certainly one of the most striking and consequential. The Persians would have prevailed easily had things gone differently at only one of perhaps a half dozen junctures. At both Salamis and Plataea, they squandered huge tactical advantages by attacking under adverse conditions; and in both cases they needn't have attacked at all, seeing that the Greek alliance might easily have been destroyed by internal divisions. A Greek looking back on the course of the war from a distance of some fifty years might easily conclude, as does a Corinthian ambassador in a speech reported by Thucydides, that the barbarians had lost the war more than the Hellenes had won it (1.69). But Herodotus instead stresses the ways in which the Greeks, through courage, intelligence, and a seemingly heaven-sent good fortune, had followed up on the opportunities that Persian errors created. In his portrayal, both sides appear to be caught up in a single paroxysm of historical change, a violent and unexpected turning of the tide. The balance of power between Europe and Asia had suddenly been reversed, altering in a single year the pattern of the past century and establishing a new pattern for centuries to come.

XI CHARACTERS AND CHARACTERIZATION

THE CAST OF CHARACTERS IN THE *HISTORIES* NUMBERS ABOUT A thousand, nearly the same as in Homer's *Iliad;* in Herodotus, as in Homer, most of that cast are bit players, mentioned but once or twice in a vast span of narrative. Sometimes, though, even these minor characters are surprisingly well captured by Herodotus. The mute son of Croesus, whose part is so small he is not even named, makes an indelible impression when his love for his father prompts him to speak his first words, commanding an attacking Persian, "You there, don't kill Croesus!" (1.85). But Herodotus, like Homer, made fully detailed portraits of only a few individuals, and it is these main characters that stand out as the great achievements and, in one or two cases, the great enigmas of his text.

In giving depth of character to his historical figures, Herodotus faced a task not unlike the one Homer had confronted some three centuries earlier. The outlines of the heroic type, the man of force (usually but not, as we shall see, inevitably male) who dominates on the battlefield or in palace halls, were already clearly limned by mythic tradition long before these authors came on the scene. The same was true, moreover, of the wily trickster or rogue, the less noble but equally compelling breed of hero represented by Homer's Odysseus and Herodotus's Themistocles. If either author had followed too closely these long-established templates, his narrative would have quickly become lifeless and oppressive, no matter how exciting the events portrayed. This peril has beset many modern movies based on Greek myth (*Clash of the Titans* is a good example): the failure to free heroes from their traditional paradigms results in an exceedingly dull script. Heracles plays the strongman, pure and simple; Zeus embodies monarchal power; Athena personifies sober wisdom, and so on. No matter how unusual or colorful the plot of such films, they bore us to tears if their characters remain only as complicated as the actions they perform.

In the *Iliad,* to look for a moment longer at that most influential of Herodotus's models, Homer took the basic character type of the man of force and created an array of unique and complex individuals. He made none so typical or straightforward as to be incapable of surprising us from time to time. Agamemnon is not like his brother Menelaus, though both are kings and stout warriors; they speak differently and fight differently, and the poet uses different kinds of similes to illustrate their actions. None of the Greeks at Troy are remotely like Achilles, though all share, to varying degrees, the warlike spirit that enables him to slaughter his enemies on the field of battle. In fact, Homer delights in the distinctions between these characters, showing us the unique fighting styles of each in a series of solo performances known to scholars by their Greek name, *aristeia.* What is more, he reveals their differing personalities in their interactions with one another, and in particular tests them each against the great touchstone of the poem, Achilles. In the embassy scene of book 9, for example, in which three of the Greek heroes try to persuade their champion to return to the fighting, Homer holds up each personality in turn to the harsh glare of Achilles' uncompromising absolutism.

Herodotus in the *Histories* works with a character type as clearly fixed by tradition as the man of force who dominates the *Iliad:* the Asian autocrat. It would have been easy for Herodotus, as it is for us today, to conjure up the basic elements of this type. Indeed, the Persian artists who carved the relief portraits of Darius and Xerxes at Persepolis, still standing today among the building's ruins, conveyed them easily enough: sumptuous robes, a tall throne, muscular bodies depicted in larger scale than that of the figures who surround them. Never mind that the faces of these figures are nearly expressionless and their features indistinguishable from the other Persians in the scene; their power and position define them, and that is enough. But it was not enough for Herodotus, whose eastern potentates are much more than simply the embodiments of royal stature. Though all have certain typical features in common, what is finally remarkable about them are the differences in the ways they wield power or subdue their enemies. Their styles of leadership can vary dramatically, as illustrated by a Persian saying that Herodotus quotes: Cyrus ruled like a father, Cambyses like a tyrant or slavemaster, and the crafty, bureaucracy-minded Darius like a merchant or shopkeeper (3.89).

In some cases, moreover, Herodotus was interested not only in the differing leadership styles of his kings, but in the lives they lead outside the central arenas of rule and conquest. For example, if one compares the portrayals of Croesus of Lydia and Cyrus of Persia, the kings whose stories are told in the first two segments of the *Histories,* one feels the presence of a fully realized human being in the first case, a statue or monument in the second. Croesus interests Herodotus not merely because of his role in the history of the East, but because of his emotions, his thoughts and attitudes, even his family relationships—what we today might call his personal life. Cyrus, by contrast, remains enshrined in the public role to which Persian legend had assigned him; we see him only through his actions in the political and military realm, and indeed rarely hear him speak, except, interestingly enough, when he engages in dialogue with Croesus. Much the same contrast might be drawn between Darius and Xerxes, the Persian emperors who are onstage, successively, for about a third of the *Histories* each. Darius, though central to the story of Persian development and expansion, remains a remote, opaque figure, his inner life largely unexplored, his speaking voice largely unheard. His son Xerxes, by contrast, seems to be always talking, revealing his deepest emotions to his uncle Artabanus or to other confidants he adopts during his invasion of Greece. Xerxes and Croesus stand, at opposite ends of the *Histories*, as Herodotus's two richest and most fully human creations, bracketing many smaller and less complex portraits between.

We are introduced to Croesus as a man of legendary wealth and power, someone who can contemplate extending his dominion over the neighboring Greeks (1.27) and who can arrogantly dismiss the precepts of the wise Solon (1.33). But after this opening episode Herodotus moves quickly to a story that reveals a gentler and more private side of the Lydian's character, the tale of his loss of a beloved son, Atys. Croesus must lose this son because, as Herodotus informs us at the tale's outset, the gods have determined that he will suffer for thinking himself the happiest of men. But the story is told as a drama rather than as a parable, filled with convincing dialogue between father and son as Croesus attempts to ward off the death he has foreseen in his dream. Once the boy has been slain, moreover, Croesus's grief is real; it causes him to cry out, Job-like, upon Zeus, the god who normally sanctifies the relation of guest and host but who in this case had allowed it to become cruelly perverted. The bereft Croesus will go on to mourn two full years for his lost son, before the rise of Cyrus and the Persians rouses him from grief—and allows Herodotus to return the narrative to the sphere of public affairs. Yet the image of Croesus as protective father established in the Atys episode continues to be subtly reinforced by Herodotus in his other accounts of the Lydian's adventures. Cyrus of Persia, for example, at one point acknowledges that Croesus had been "something more than a father to the Lydians" (1.155) and regrets that he had "orphaned" them by depriving them of their ruler.

Croesus's decision to stand up to the growing Persian threat forces him to become an aggressor and a battlefield general, not an easy role for a good father to play; for, as Croesus himself will proclaim, "No one is so foolish as to prefer war to peace, for in peace sons bury their fathers, while in war fathers bury their sons" (1.87). Indeed, Croesus prepares for the campaign in a strangely nonaggressive way, seeking to guarantee victory in advance by securing a reliable forecast from a Greek oracle (1.46–55). His faith in this magical solution leads him to disregard even the most elementary of tactical principles, so that he attacks with an army smaller than that of the defending Persians (1.77). Thus comes about the first failed invasion of the *Histories*, a work that will largely be concerned with failed invasions: each successive leader reveals his own peculiar style in the way he conducts an attack, and the cautious, calculating, risk-averse style of Croesus is particularly distinctive. By contrast, the manner in which Cyrus counterinvades Lydia (and in which his subsequent conquests throughout book 1 are undertaken) is bold and direct, the risk-embracing spirit of a true warrior-king. The pairing of Croesus and Cyrus as the first two major figures of the *Histories*, whose unparallel lives are recounted in nearly symmetrical "halves" of what we now know as book 1, invites us to draw such comparisons between their military careers. Ironically, though, Cyrus will end his career—and his life—by adopting the "covert operations" approach urged on him by Croesus at a critical strategic juncture (1.207).

An even more striking contrast emerges in book 3, in which Croesus becomes guardian to one of Herodotus's most compelling characters, Cyrus's son Cambyses. Next to the sober, sage, paternal Croesus—a man now around seventy years old, to judge by the chronology of the *Histories*—Cambyses comes across as a hot-blooded, ill-mannered, arrogant youth. In the face of his ward's violent excesses, Croesus becomes a virtual embodiment of temperate humanity, as seen on the first occasion when Herodotus puts the two men onstage together. Cambyses, having conquered Egypt in one blow, subjects the vanquished pharaoh Psammenitus to a cruel psychological torture: he forces the fallen king to watch his son and daughter march past in a parade of young men bound for execution and women bound for slavery. But Psammenitus looks on impassively and gives way to grief only when he spies an elderly drinking companion marching in the procession of captives. After he explains to Cambyses, through an interpreter, that his own family's sufferings had been too great for tears, Herodotus reports,

> As the Egyptians say, Croesus cried (for he too happened to have followed Cambyses into Egypt), and those of the Persians who were present cried also; and a certain pity stole upon Cambyses himself, and he ordered his men to save Psammenitus's son from those being executed . . . and to bring the pharaoh himself to his side. (3.14)

Those noble tears of Croesus speak volumes, coming from a former king who has himself stood upon a burning pyre at the whim of a Persian conqueror. And remarkably, they have the power to move even Cambyses to pity, a man who commits abuses in Egypt as savage as any atrocities of modern warfare.

Cambyses occupies the stage of the *Histories* for only a brief time, yet he leaves the most vivid impression of any of

Herodotus's Persians; as in Shakespeare's *Richard III*, an embodiment of pure malignant violence compels our attention more easily than characters of mixed or moderate parts. Yet Herodotus, himself a person of large and forgiving humanity, handles Cambyses' lawlessness with sympathy, seeking, in one important aside, to understand its cause:

> Cambyses committed these insane deeds against his own household, whether as a result of [his killing of the] Apis or for some other reason; for many are the evils that are wont to befall humankind. For indeed Cambyses is said to have had a serious illness from birth, the one that some call the sacred disease. It would not be at all unlikely if, when there is a serious illness of the body present, the mind of the sick man is also unwell. (3.33)

After Cambyses' madness lifts, Herodotus actually ennobles him by giving him a penitent deathbed speech and allowing him to move the assembled Persians to tears, as Croesus had done earlier (3.65–66). Where Cambyses might have been demonized, that is, Herodotus instead depicts the tragic condition of a man driven by disease or madness to turn away from the biddings of humanity but returning to them when, in his last moments, he recovers his senses. In this world, as in Homer's (where even the bestial Cyclops is handled sympathetically), there are no mere monsters, and no human villains beyond redemption.

Along with tragic figures like Croesus and Cambyses, whose nobility lies in their sufferings and their ability to feel those of others, Herodotus also presents a comic model of kingship in the Egyptian pharaoh Amasis. Our introduction to this lively character, in chapter 162 of book 2 (there have been but incidental references to him before this), shows him behaving in a manner unthinkable for the other kings portrayed in the *Histories* and more appropriate for the hero of an Aristophanic farce. Amasis is at this point a king in name only, having been summarily crowned by a group of Egyptian rebels whom the true pharaoh, Apries, had sent him to negotiate with. When Apries learns of his desertion and sends a messenger to summon him back, Amasis, seated on horseback, grandly arises and breaks wind, bidding the envoy to "take *that* back to Apries." With this childlike act of defiance, Amasis begins his usurpation of the throne and a reign of forty-four years, ending just before the conquest of Egypt by Cambyses and the Persians—forty-four years, as Herodotus informs us, in which no great evils befell him (3.10).

The Egyptians at first show little esteem for their new pharaoh, who, unlike his predecessors, had arisen from the common people. But Amasis wins them over by again displaying his flair for scatological wit. Taking apart a golden vessel that had been used as a footbath and chamber pot, Amasis constructs out of it a statue of a god and places it where the public can worship it. When he sees the Egyptians paying reverence to the statue, he points out that he, too, had risen from the lowest social order to the highest, and in this way wins them over, as Herodotus says approvingly, "with cleverness, not with willful pride" (2.172). This cleverness, or *sophiē,* is a quality Amasis shares with his contemporary, the Athenian lawgiver Solon (1.30), and indeed, Herodotus brings these two leaders into juxtaposition on two occasions (1.30, 2.177). And as we have seen, Amasis is made to echo the moral wisdom of Solon when he writes to the tyrant Polycrates in book 3, bidding him beware the jealousy of the gods (chapter 40).

The lively, irreverent spirit that Amasis displays in his flatulent entrance onto the political scene continues to manifest itself throughout his reign. Herodotus tells us that Amasis had liked to drink, joke, and carouse before his accession and that he refused to give these pleasures up after assuming the throne; rather, he reserved his mornings for affairs of state, then in the afternoons and evenings turned back to his frat-boy ways. To those grave counselors who urge him to adopt a more lofty demeanor, Amasis replies with a parable as memorable as that of the golden footbath: "Men who own bows string them when they need to, and unstring them when they don't. If they were strung all the time they would break, and their owners couldn't use them when there was need. Such, also, is the nature of a man. If he should always be in earnest and never indulge any part of himself in play, he would, unbeknownst to himself, go mad or become stricken. But I, who understand this, allot due measure to each pursuit" (2.173). In this way Amasis manages to refashion the kingship after his own image and to remain a merry prankster, a Prince Hal unwilling to grow up into Henry V, even on the throne of Egypt.

Not many characters in the *Histories* share Amasis's humble origins or brassy style; like the Athenian tragedies and Homeric epics on which it is partly modeled, the book concerns itself principally with the highborn and lofty, people of sober or grave demeanor. But Herodotus also has a sharp eye and, one feels, a warm affection for the "little people" who occasionally get drawn into the world of tyrants and kings. Often these minor characters are Greeks, and Herodotus delights in showing us the cleverness, sangfroid, and unconcealed eagerness for profit they display in their dealings with eastern potentates. The physician Democedes of Croton, for example, plays the wily trickster when trapped at the court of Darius, manipulating the emperor's wife into arranging a means for his escape (3.130–37). After finally gaining his freedom and making off with a shipload of royal gifts into the bargain, Democedes, like Odysseus escaping from Homer's Cyclops, cannot resist hurling a boast at his former captor: he sends a message to Darius that he intends to marry a famous man's daughter and thus become a "big shot" in his own right (3.137). A similar spirit of plucky self-interest is shown by Alcmaeon, who, when offered a gift of as much of Croesus's wealth as he could carry, puts on a suit of clothes baggy enough to rival Harpo Marx's famous raincoat and stuffs every pocket, and finally even his mouth, with gold (6.125). Croesus could only laugh at the balloonish figure that waddled out of his treasure-house; and Herodotus seems to join in this laughter, to enjoy the adventures of the comic Everyman as an interlude to weightier tales of the high and mighty. Although many of his episodes reveal the influence of tragic dramas, Herodotus had no doubt also learned a lesson or two from the bawdy, ebullient satyr plays that always accompanied the tragedies in their original performances.

The character of Xerxes, explored in books 7 through 9 of the *Histories*, might easily have been the weightiest and most deeply tragic portrait of all. After all, Aeschylus, in his play *The Persians*, had already constructed a version of Xerxes' character similar to Herodotus's portrait of Cambyses: an impetuous youth who had hurled himself headlong into a reckless fight, ungoverned by the wisdom of his elders. Such a portrayal, indeed, would have had had strong appeal to a Greek audience, whose acquaintance with Homer's *Iliad* had made the hot-blooded, intemperate youth a familiar and fascinating figure. But Herodotus chose not to follow Aeschylus's lead in this matter. Starting right from the beginning of book 7, he assigns the Iliadic role of the impetuous warrior to Xerxes' general Mardonius and makes the king himself into something less heroic but more complex: an unwarlike but dutiful bearer of the burden of rule. In Herodotus's view, Xerxes, far from having defied Darius's wishes in mounting a new expedition into

Europe, had actually inherited his father's war and carried it
on despite his own inclinations; like Croesus in book 1, he finds
himself forced to play the aggressor, though temperamentally
ill-suited to this part.

Herodotus makes clear from the start that Xerxes, upon
assuming the throne in 486, did not want to carry out Darius's
plan for a second invasion of Greece (7.5). He had already seen
two earlier attempts, Mardonius's foray of 492 and the landing
at Marathon two years later, come to grief. Perhaps a more self-
confident king could have scuttled the plan, even in the tentative early years of his reign, but Xerxes is no such king. No
sooner has he assumed power than he allows his ambitious
cousin Mardonius, who stands to gain by the invasion, to coax
him into seeing it through, rather than settling for his own
more limited goal of reconquering tractable Egypt (7.5–6). In
his speech announcing the invasion plan to the Persian nobility,
Xerxes at first seems every inch a king; but when his own ad-
dress is immediately followed by one from Mardonius "smoothing over the opinion of Xerxes," as Herodotus says in a curious
metaphor, we are reminded that it was the elder general, not
the young monarch, who had been pressing for the invasion all
along.

When Xerxes' uncle Artabanus then speaks against the expedition, Xerxes suddenly grows enraged and berates the old
sage for cowardice. Here, perhaps, we see a flash of the youth-
ful ardor with which Aeschylus had endowed the Xerxes of
The Persians; indeed, Herodotus's Xerxes later explains his out-
burst by saying that "my youth boiled up in me" (7.13). But
we are also aware that Artabanus, in Herodotus's version of
events, is only giving voice to doubts that Xerxes himself had
felt before Mardonius set to work on him. Later that night, in
fact, those doubts return, and Xerxes abruptly changes his
mind:

> When night had fallen, the opinion of Artabanus grated on Xerxes; and after spending part of the night in calculation, he entirely made up his mind that it did not behoove him to attack Greece. (7.12)

Xerxes' youthfulness, in other words, expresses itself not as fiery aggression, as in Aeschylus's play, but as a lack of resolution when dealing with elder counselors. The king is like a sea whose nature is altered by gusts of wind, according to the memorable simile of Artabanus (7.16). In the end, his mind is made up for him by the appearance of the dream vision that demands he proceed with the invasion (see the end of chapter IX).

Herodotus brings Artabanus back into the narrative in a celebrated dialogue at the banks of the Hellespont, in order to again throw a spotlight onto Xerxes' ambivalent feelings about his new command (7.44–52). Seated on a viewing platform erected high on a hilltop, Xerxes surveys his entire army and fleet—many millions of men, by Herodotus's count—as they prepare to cross over into Europe. After a momentary surge of happiness at seeing the immense array of forces, Xerxes suddenly does something quite startling: he breaks down and weeps. "As I took the measure of this host," he explains to Artabanus, "I felt a sudden pity at how short is all of human life, since of these great numbers, not one will remain alive a hundred years hence." Artabanus, echoing the sentiments expressed in book 1 by Solon, agrees that mortal life is both evanescent and filled with pain, a gift to humanity from some jealous god. The whole exchange is framed in a sublime spirit of contemplation, at a great remove, quite literally, from the sphere of action; Herodotus here borrows from Homer's technique in the *Iliad*, whereby the Trojan War is occasionally viewed from the lofty perspective of the gods on Olympus. But Xerxes, being mortal himself, experiences the scene before him very differently from the way Homer's Olympians would: he weeps. Like Croesus, the only other ruler in the *Histories* who sheds tears, Xerxes shows himself to be a creature capable of deep and ennobling empathy.

But in the end, tears are the luxury of a spectator of history, not a participant. Xerxes abruptly ends his meditation on the brevity of human life in order to consider the matters he has in hand. Now, as though still unresolved about his earlier decision to invade, he poses a remarkable question to Artabanus: "If the dream vision had not appeared so openly, would you still hold to your old opinion and bid me not to make an attack on Greece, or would you have changed your mind?" When Artabanus admits that he does in fact still harbor some doubts, Xerxes responds,

> Artabanus, you judge all these matters reasonably; but don't fear everything or examine everything with equal scrutiny. For if, in the face of every circumstance that is advanced, you wish to scrutinize everything, you would never do anything; it's better to take courage and suffer half of the things we fear, than to dread all undertakings in advance and never undergo any experience at all. . . . You see how far the Persian empire has progressed in power. Consider then that if those kings who preceded me had formed judgments like yours . . . you would never have seen the empire advance so far; but in fact they ran the risks, and brought it thus far forward. (7.50)

These are bold words indeed, but they seem to be addressed by Xerxes as much to himself as to Artabanus; it was Xerxes, after all, who had asked for a reopening of the invasion question to begin with. The whole dialogue brilliantly portrays Xerxes taking upon himself the mantle of leadership but doing so reflectively and by cautious half-steps, more out of a sense of duty than as a result of his inclinations.

Critics have argued over whether this Xerxes can be called a tragic figure, and the question is not an easy one to answer. Certainly he does not fit the standard Greek paradigm of the tragic monarch, as represented, say, by the Xerxes of Aeschylus's play *The Persians;* at times he more closely resembles Virgil's Aeneas, a man of feeling forced by historical circumstance to become a man of action. Indeed, the tears he sheds upon seeing his forces gathered at the Hellespont anticipate Aeneas's weeping in the first book of the *Aeneid,* when he glimpses a sculptural representation of the trials he had endured in the Trojan War. Whereas Aeneas succeeds in adapting to his new military role, however, even at the cost of his humanity, Xerxes retains rather too much humanity to succeed as the conqueror of Greece. After his defeat at Salamis he departs from Europe— in a paroxysm of fear, according to Herodotus (8.103)—and thereafter the only glimpse we have of him shows him embroiled in a disastrous love affair with his own niece and daughter-in-law, Artaynte (9.108–13). Herodotus allows him no Croesus-style inquiry into the meaning of his military failure, only what seems to be a retreat from public life into the pleasures of amorous intrigue. In the end, as one interpreter of the *Histories* has written, "we have no feelings of pity or fear for this king, but merely the sense that he is, somehow, unsound."

We must not exit the great portrait gallery of the *Histories* without taking account of its female characters, who, though they do not loom large in the narrative, are nonetheless striking and memorable. In their cases, though, Herodotus has hewed rather closer than usual to the templates he inherited from the mythic tradition. For the Greeks had long been fascinated with warrior women, especially those thought to inhabit the far North and East; from these regions the legendary Amazons had come to do battle with Hellenic armies, dressed, according to the usual Greek depictions of them, in leather clothing that gave them a distinctly Asian appearance. Herodotus's own description of the Amazons, a digression from his Scythian ethnography (4.110-17), casts them not only as fearsome warriors but as high-minded feminists, unwilling to compromise their culture or give up their homeland in marriage (as most ancient women were required to do). It was perhaps inevitable, therefore, that the Amazon myth was present to Herodotus's mind when he dealt with the warrior-queens of the barbarian world, whose strength and independence made them objects of both fear and admiration to his own primarily male audience. Tomyris of the Massagetae, for example, conforms to this type when she rejects the perfidious marriage offer tendered by Cyrus (1.205) as well as when she savagely punishes Cyrus's corpse by plunging his head into a skin filled with blood (1.214).

Artemisia of Halicarnassus, the warrior-queen who accompanies Xerxes' invasion as captain of a contingent of ships, presents us with a refined and Hellenized version of the Amazon type. Like the goddess Artemis for whom she is named, she stands separate from, but equal to, the male hierarchy that ordinarily dominates the military arena. Herodotus specifies, in a chapter of his catalogue of Persian forces in which he singles her out as a *thōma*, or marvel, that she served in Xerxes' army not under compulsion but motivated by sheer fighting spirit and "manly courage," *andrēiē* (7.99). The noun *andrēiē*, derived from a word for "male" and used only here in the *Histories*, clearly has ironic point when applied to a woman, and Herodotus follows up on this irony in two subsequent episodes connected with the battle of Salamis. Before the battle has begun, Artemisia warns Xerxes to avoid a direct confrontation with the Greek navy because "these [Greek] men are as much better than yours on the sea as men are than women" (8.68). Later, when Artemisia performs a bold maneuver in the heat of battle even as the other Persian ships falter, Xerxes, looking on from a high hilltop, exclaims, "My men have become women, my women men" (8.88). In all three passages, Herodotus casts Artemisia as an Amazonian androgyne, a female whose temperament and nature seem to identify her closely with males— so much so that she herself can speak disparagingly of women as creatures inferior to men.

It is interesting that Artemisia wins the trust of Xerxes and serves as his closest advisor in the agonizing aftermath of Salamis, as the king contemplates whether to remain with his army in Europe or sail for the Hellespont (8.101–3). Perhaps it would be assuming too much psychological sophistication on Herodotus's part to suggest that Xerxes, the male leader who reveals certain behaviors more typical of a woman, finds his natural complement in the figure of a woman who is more like a man. However that may be, there is something touching and convincing about the affinity of these two characters, as seen in the unusual private colloquy Herodotus stages between them following Salamis. Herodotus reports, in his final notice concerning Artemisia, that she conveyed Xerxes' illegitimate children home from the war (8.103, 107)—the Amazon warrior retiring from battle to become the royal nanny!

XII PERSIANS AND GREEKS

ON THE OCCASIONS IN POST-CLASSICAL TIMES WHEN ASIAN peoples have invaded Europe—the Huns in the fifth century, the Mongols or Tatars in the thirteenth, the Turks in the sixteenth—they have appeared to those who stood in their path as subhuman savages or as devils loosed out of Hell. The Tatars, for example, were identified by medieval Europeans with the monstrous races of Gog and Magog whom Alexander the Great had supposedly locked behind mountain gates in central Asia and whose irruption into the Christian world signaled the coming of the Apocalypse. The first Europeans to have seen them face-to-face described them as follows, in the words of the chronicler Matthew Paris: "They are inhuman and beastly, rather monsters than men, thirsting for and drinking blood, tearing and devouring the flesh of dogs and men. . . . They are without human laws, know no comforts, are more ferocious than lions or bears." Later, after the Mongol threat to Europe had passed, Marco Polo would give a more positive and even admiring report of the empire of Kublai Khan, but few contemporary readers believed him; images of cannibalism and bestiality had become fixed in the Christian mind and were not easily dispelled. Indeed, the word "Tatar," as well as "Hun" and "Turk," came to signify, in European languages, a person of wild, cruel, and disorderly ways, someone who not only stood beyond the bounds of the civilized world but whose very existence threatened to turn that world upside down.

In ancient Greece, neither racial nor religious attitudes were conducive to this kind of demonization, even after an Asian intruder had penetrated to the very heart of the Hellenic homelands. Postinvasion paintings and sculptures of the Persians, for example the marble figures in the frieze on the Nike temple in Athens (see chapter XIII), depicted a noble race whose odd-looking leather clothes did not betoken any moral inferiority. Indeed, the prevailing Greek tendency was to elevate the stature of the Persians rather than debase it, thereby making the struggles of 490 and 480–79 seem a more heroic effort: as in the Trojan War glorified by Homer's *Iliad*, the Greeks had faced the most noble peoples of Asia and had won. More remarkable still is the notion put forward in Aeschylus's play *The Persians*, written only eight years after the battle of Salamis, that the struggle between Greece and Persia had been a quarrel not only of moral equals but of *sisters*. At the opening of this play, Atossa, mother of Xerxes, describes a dream she has had that prefigures, in symbolic terms, the course of the war then in progress: two sisters, one dressed in Persian robes, the other in Doric (that is, in the style of European Greece), had fallen to quarreling; Xerxes had tried to yoke them, and one accepted the bridle, but the other broke loose and tore the king's chariot to pieces. Not only are the leading peoples of Asia and Europe here portrayed as siblings, but both are described as tall and strikingly beautiful, different in dress but not in stature.

If neither race nor religion established for the Greeks the kind of "continental divide" later constructed by Christian Europe, however, politics was a different matter. Asia under the Persian empire was ruled by a king, the Great King as the Greeks called him, who seemed to embody the very concept of monarchal power; whereas European Greece, by the fifth century, had largely thrown off monarchy or autocracy of any kind in favor of more pluralistic systems like oligarchy and democracy. The dream image of Aeschylus's *Persians*, in which the Asian sister willingly takes the bridle and bit Xerxes thrusts upon her while the Greek sister rejects it, is freighted with political symbolism: Asia had submitted to its monarch like beasts of burden to a master, passively and without protest, whereas Greece had struggled to remain free. Later in the play the same idea recurs, expressed again in animal imagery, when Atossa, eager to know more about the people her son has attacked, idly asks the chorus, "Who is the herdsman or overlord of their forces?" to which the chorus replies, "They are reputed to be neither the slaves nor subjects of anyone" (lines 241–42). Aeschylus here has Atossa casually use the term "herdsman," as if to suggest that, within her culture, it was natural to conceive of a ruler's dominion over his subjects as analogous to that of humanity over the beasts. Finally, in a choral ode sung by the elders of Persia yet expressing, from behind the mask, a Hellenic point of view, Aeschylus celebrates the defeat of Xerxes at Salamis as the downfall of this political ideology:

> Dwellers along Asian land
> are Persian-ruled no longer,
> nor any longer bear tribute
> at the compulsion of masters,
> nor lie prone on the ground
> in subservience, since royal power
> has been destroyed. (586–92)

The overthrow of Xerxes' power is here seen as the end both of enslavement and of *proskunēsis*, the ceremonial self-prostration demanded by Persian royalty of their subjects and detested, on moral and religious grounds, by the Greeks.

But if Aeschylus thus gives voice to a typically Greek mistrust of monarchy in some passages of *The Persians*, he also brings on stage the ghost of a wise and just monarch, Xerxes' father, Darius. It was Darius, as Aeschylus and his audience well knew, who had made the Persian empire a great and well-run state; and even though the historical Darius had also ordered the first Persian assault on mainland Greece and laid plans for the second, he appears in *The Persians* as an opponent of his son's expansionism and an advocate of moderation and restraint. Such a characterization served Aeschylus's artistic purposes, in that it throws the impetuosity of his tragic hero, Xerxes, into high relief. But it also clouds whatever political message might otherwise have been derived from the play. Monarchy cannot, in the end, be regarded as an absolute moral evil because history reveals good monarchs as well as bad; a string of Dariuses able to learn from their errors and curb their ambitions might have made the Persian empire an ideal political system.

Herodotus, like Aeschylus, was more artist and dramatist than political thinker, and as a result the *Histories* does not easily yield up universal or consistent principles of good government. For Herodotus, too, analyses of political systems are always contingent on the characters of those who take part in them, and assessments of kingship vary as widely as the personalities of kings. Scholars have disagreed even over the basic questions of whether Herodotus disapproved of Asian hereditary monarchy or its nearest analogue in the mainland Greek world, tyranny (an institution that Herodotus sometimes calls "monarchy" or "kingship," seemingly assimilating it to the constitutional brand of one-man rule that prevailed in Persia), or what his attitude was toward the system at the opposite end of the political spectrum, Athenian democracy. These questions now deserve a closer look, even if, as is so often the case for readers of the *Histories,* no simple or definitive answers are possible.

An obvious place to begin is the so-called Debate on Government in book 3 (chapters 80–82), a passage in which Herodotus tries his hand at a kind of discourse that Plato and Aristotle would later develop into a full-fledged philosophy of politics. Here, more than anywhere else in the *Histories,* the three systems of government known to the Greeks—monarchy, oligarchy, and democracy—are examined in the abstract, rather than in the particular contexts of the world's many nations and states. Here, more than anywhere else, one would hope to gain insight into Herodotus's own political leanings, given that the three analyses are almost certainly his own creations—although he represents them as speeches delivered by a group of Persian nobles as they prepare to seize the throne and install a new regime. What we find, however, is that the author remains completely neutral, giving a full and convincing airing of the case for and, mostly, against each of the major systems. First, Otanes decries the recklessness and vanity of monarchs, who trample on their worthy subjects and surround themselves with toadies and flatterers; only democracy, he claims, can protect the rights of the individual against such abuses. But, objects Megabyzus, government by the people becomes mob rule, driven by the passions and prejudices of unschooled masses; only the few best men know how to manage public affairs. Nevertheless, says Darius, the jealous rivalries of those best men lead them into factionalism, until finally they destroy one another; or else they club together to promote their own interests and cheat the masses. In either case, Darius maintains, a single strongman eventually emerges to set things right, and under this "one best man" the best sort of government takes shape. As a final argument, Darius reminds his comrades of their own history: it was Cyrus, the great exemplar of absolute rule, who had led the revolt against the Medes and so given the Persians their freedom.

At this point, the debate is ended and a vote is held, and all three of the "neutrals" among those present support Darius and monarchy. In other words, we witness the phenomenon, paradoxical to citizens of a modern democracy, of a people voting freely and fairly to disenfranchise themselves of political rights. But Herodotus says nothing that implies disapproval of this choice, just as he does nothing to skew the arguments in the debate toward one system or another. In addition, by allowing Darius to claim *eleutheriē*, "freedom," as one of the benefits of monarchy, Herodotus reveals how complex and contingent political analyses can become: only through the leadership of a king had the Persians overthrown the rule of the Medes, so as to enjoy not only autonomy but the overlordship of all Asia. That is, Herodotus allows a pragmatic, non-ideological argument to tilt the scales in an otherwise equal contest: autocracy wins the day among the Persians because, by and large, it had *worked*, increasing the power and prestige of each member of the society.

The Debate on Government expresses in concise form the political viewpoint of the entire *Histories*, a work that finds both strengths and weaknesses in each of the major systems of government and ultimately stands more on the side of pragmatism than ideology. Whether looking at democratic Athens or monarchic Persia or Sparta—whose constitution was a mixture of different elements, not easily classifiable—Herodotus shows us both what works and what fails; no system is free from problems, and none is without merit. And though he does in the end frame the conflict between Greece and Persia as a political struggle, as we shall see, his attitude toward government follows the same relativistic principles we observed in his discussion of culture: each nation, given the chance, would choose its own over others, and custom rules over all.

The fact remains, though, that Asia, in the period covered by the *Histories*, had chosen monarchy, while Greece for the most part was in the process of throwing out its tyrants and establishing the rule of law. Herodotus explores this political distinction between the continents as eagerly as he does their geographic separation (see chapter VI). One-man rule, though neither good nor bad in itself, is indigenous to the nations of the East, whereas in the Greek *poleis* it often has to be established by force among an unwilling populace. In book 1, for example, Herodotus illustrates in some detail the founding of both a Greek tyranny and an Asian monarchy, and the comparison is revealing. At Athens, the tyrant Pisistratus wins power by trickery and preserves it by force. He surrounds himself first with a corps of club-wielding native bodyguards and later with foreign mercenaries; evidently the effect he achieved by having a woman dressed to look like Athena proclaim his rule (1.60) did not protect him for long. Twice his subjects expel him from the city, and twice he wins his way back, resorting in the end to the grim measure of taking hostages from leading Athenian families (1.64). In all respects his sovereignty in Athens is like an occupation by a foreign power, as Herodotus himself indicates when he says that the city was "held" by Pisistratus (1.59), using a word (*katechomenon*) that usually connotes domination from without.

By contrast, the start of Deioces' kingship in Asia is portrayed by Herodotus (1.96–101) as a natural and peaceful process, freely chosen, like the monarchy in Persia, by the people themselves. Prior to this, the Medes had enjoyed political autonomy but their society had degenerated into lawlessness and disorder; Deioces comes to the fore as a kind of Wyatt Earp, bringing the rule of law to a chaotic land. The Medes elect him as their king, whereupon he asks not only for a bodyguard but for a vast and stoutly fortified palace surrounded by seven concentric walls. Within this forbidding complex Deioces hides himself from view, surrounding his kingship with an air of gravity and mystery that serves as his shield against opposition. Whereas Pisistratus had succeeded only briefly in making Athena appear to be his patroness, Deioces finds a more long-lasting method of instilling in his subjects a sense of his super-human stature.

Pisistratus's stage-Athena ruse strikes Herodotus as the kind of thing a barbarian, not a Greek, would swallow (1.60), so he finds nothing remarkable in Deioces' ability to overawe his fellow Medes. Indeed, the mystification of the king's person and office serves Herodotus as one of the defining features of Asian monarchy, in contrast to the more limited forms of hereditary rule still surviving in archaic Greece. The ritual of *proskunēsis*, for example, the prostration of the lowborn before the high, is described by Herodotus as a custom deeply in-grained in Persian society (1.134); later, he recounts an episode in which a pair of Spartan envoys refuse, at peril of their lives, to perform this obeisance before Xerxes on the grounds that it befits gods, not men (7.136). The Persian kings, following the model established by Deioces the Mede, maintain power by blurring the lines between monarch and deity, whereas the Greeks insist on maintaining this boundary, and the few Greek rulers who try to cross it are soon exposed as frauds. For example, in a long account of the rivalries between dual kings at Sparta, Herodotus recounts how Demaratus was thrust from power by his coregent Cleomenes after questions had arisen about the legitimacy of Demaratus's birth (6.61 ff.). Though a story circulating at the time made Demaratus seem the son of a god, the Spartans found it more credible that he was simply a bastard, perhaps even, as Cleomenes and his faction claimed, the offspring of a mule driver.

Lacking the aura of mystery that surrounds eastern monarchies, the tyrannies of Greece have less security against their foes when, as inevitably happens, a less competent son inherits rule from his powerful father. Interestingly, both of the tyrannies whose progress Herodotus follows closely, the Pisistratid dynasty in Athens and the Cypselids of Corinth, seem destined to end in the second generation: Cypselus is told by the oracle at Delphi that he and his sons will have good fortune, but not the sons of his sons (5.92), and Hipparchus, son of Pisistratus and brother to the reigning Hippias, foresees in a dream his own assassination—an event that precipitates the overthrow of the dynasty (5.55–56). In both cases, as we know from the *Histories* and from other sources, the children of the founding tyrant became fearful or avaricious after they assumed power and alienated the people by their cruelty. Herodotus makes no inquiry why this should be so, though it is interesting to note that his Persian kings follow a similar pattern: noble Cyrus begets sadistic, paranoid Cambyses, whose excesses spark a palace coup; sure-footed Darius begets stumbling Xerxes, who manages to hold the throne but only (as indicated in a final anecdote, 9.108–13) by killing off would-be usurpers. Modern-day political observers, who have witnessed the same generational sequence in autocracies like Haiti and North Korea, might turn to developmental psychology to explain the inadequacy of these sons of great men, but Herodotus knows no such science. In any case, the short duration of these two Greek tyrannies contrasts sharply with the dynasties of Lydia, Media, and Egypt, which typically last either four or five generations and do not seem to degenerate over time; and even in Persia the Achaemenid family soon regains the throne lost by Cambyses.

What is more, in the examples Herodotus focuses on, exiled tyrants in the Greek world are replaced not by new tyrants, but by constitutional regimes. (Polycrates, tyrant of Samos, is a somewhat different case; his overthrow is engineered from without by the Persians, who replace him with his more tractable brother, Syloson.) Here, too, Herodotus draws a bright line between Asian and European political life or, more particularly, between Persia and Greece. The monarchic regime in Persia is to some extent limited by law (not even the Great King can order summary executions, 1.137), and its power is circumscribed by the nobles who lead its armed forces. But when Cambyses, for example, defies both his nobles and his laws, the rules are rewritten to suit him: his royal judges proclaim a new statute that "he who rules the Persians can do whatever he wishes" (3.31). In a system that elevates the kingship above the human plane, the will of the individual ruler always supersedes the force of an impersonal *nomos* (law or custom). By contrast, the balance of power in the Greek world inclines toward *nomos*, even though strong individuals may temporarily disrupt that balance. Sparta, with its legendary *eunomia*, or "sound law code," allegedly handed down by Lycurgus, exemplifies in the *Histories* a constitutional government that was proof against scheming kings, including Cleomenes (6.74–84) and, after the war's end, Pausanias (5.32). Indeed, although Herodotus's portrait of internal Spartan affairs may strike readers as fractious and messy, it serves to show how a stable regime weathers its crises, even during a major war, without a disruption of time-honored *eunomia*.

To underscore the contrast between the rule of law in Greece and the rule of men in Asia, Herodotus allows an exiled Spartan king, Demaratus, to serve as commentator on Xerxes' invasion and to have an important dialogue with Xerxes just before the battle of Thermopylae. The imaginary (one supposes) conversation is staged as though Herodotus were pausing, in the moments before the first clash of arms, to explore the differences in outlook between the leading powers on either side. Xerxes begins by asking Demaratus whether the Greeks will stand and fight against his vastly more numerous army. Demaratus answers him on behalf of the Spartans, though his words apply in some measure to the Hellenic world as a whole: toughened by poverty and inspired by sound laws, these men will never submit. Xerxes laughs at his presumption and demands a more realistic answer:

> How could a thousand, or ten thousand, or fifty thousand men, all being free and equal and not under a single commander, stand up to such a great army? . . . If they were all ruled by one man, according to *our* way, they might fear him and become better than their own nature, and advance, under compulsion of the whip, though few against many; but with freedom permitted to them, they could not do either of these things.

To which Demaratus replies, in one of the most stirring utterances in the *Histories,*

> Though free, they are not altogether free; for law [*nomos*] stands as master [*despotēs*] over them, and they fear it much more than your men fear you. They do whatever it orders them to do, and it always orders the same thing: It forbids them to flee from even a host of men in battle, but to stay in position and either prevail or die. (7.103–4)

—at which point Xerxes, perhaps not fully understanding what he has been told, laughs genially and sends Demaratus away.

Despotēs nomos, "law/custom is master" or even "slave-master," is a hard saying, a more severe version of Herodotus's own pronouncement on culture in book 3, *nomos basileus,* "law/custom is king." But then the Spartans are a hard people, for otherwise they could not stand unmoved, as they will shortly do, in the face of certain death. Moreover, Demaratus's phrase resonates with another earlier passage in the *Histories*, in which we are told that the Persians called their ruler Cambyses a *despotēs* "because he was bitter and scornful" (3.89). The king who had bent law to his will is implicitly contrasted with a rule of law that towers even over kings—for this same Demaratus, we recall, had earlier been removed from royal office as the result of a legal proceeding, despite the myth of his divine parentage.

Herodotus clearly stands on the side of Demaratus and of Greek political culture generally in this moving dialogue, and throughout the last three books of the *Histories*, in which that culture triumphs over autocracy. But lest we be tempted to make an ideology out of his sympathy, we should note that Herodotus also refuses to portray the Greco-Persian conflict purely as a war of liberation or to give up his cherished cultural relativism even where hot-button issues of subjection and autonomy were concerned. True, Xerxes might seem at first glance a bully or dictator, when in the above passage he insists that an army be "ruled by one man" (*hup' henos archomenoi*)—even when this requires the force of the whip. But when we recall what Herodotus had said earlier about the Thracians, using noticeably similar language, we see the other side of the coin:

> The Thracian nation is the largest of all humankind, after the Indians. If they could be ruled by one man [*hup' henos archoito*], or if they could make common cause, they would be unbeatable in war and by far the most powerful of all peoples, according to my view. But this is impossible for them, and cannot by any means be brought about. So as a result they are weak. (5.3)

The overcentralization of Asia here finds its antithesis in the divisiveness and disorganization of barbarian Europe—a condition Herodotus seems very much to regret. Xerxes' stern methods may not look attractive, but we are reminded at several points in the *Histories* that without them, the Persians might not have won their empire.

Military prowess is one gauge by which to evaluate a system of government, though certainly not the best, as recent history has demonstrated. Nevertheless, that is the yardstick Herodotus applies in his one explicit assessment of the democracy in Athens, a regime that came to birth after the fall of the Pisistratid tyranny and grew ever more vibrant in the period of the Persian Wars. The advent of this unique political system, previously all but unknown in the Greek world (or elsewhere for that matter), invited authorial comment, and Herodotus takes the opportunity directly after describing the unprecedented military triumphs of post-Pisistratid Athens. Referring to the new democracy under the label *isēgoriē*, "equal rights of speech," he praises it as the key to Athens's newfound strength:

> Not only in this one instance, but everywhere, it's clear that *isēgoriē* is an excellent thing, since when the Athenians were ruled by tyrants they never proved better in warfare than those surrounding them, but once rid of the tyrants they became by far the foremost. This shows that while they were oppressed they played the slacker in battle, since they were toiling only for a master, but once freed, each man was eager to achieve things on his own behalf. (5.78)

Athenian democracy here wins Herodotus's approval because it unleashes the self-interest of its citizens and makes them better warriors—much as American democracy is today esteemed by many merely as a place where capitalist entrepreneurs can make their fortunes. Indeed, the pragmatism behind this remark recalls Darius's final comment on monarchy in the Debate on Government: the best system is the one that had *worked*, bringing an increase in national power and prestige. As for the moral virtues that democracy might be thought to foster, the qualities portrayed by Thucydides, for instance, in the famous funeral oration of Pericles, Herodotus is notably silent about them. And in terms of democracy's ability to govern wisely, Herodotus seems to share some of Megabyzus's doubts about the rule of unlettered masses: a few chapters after the above passage, when Athens first chooses to support the revolt of the Ionians from Persia, Herodotus sneers that "it seems to be easier to deceive many people than one" (meaning King Cleomenes of Sparta, who had declined to aid the rebels, 5.97).

Athenian history gave Herodotus an opportunity to eulogize liberty and autonomy in their most highly advanced form, had he chosen to do so. Instead, the premiere democracy in the Greek world comes to represent not freedom, but a very different set of values: scrappiness, innovation, and ambitious pursuit of power. That is to say, Herodotus declines to make Athenian democracy the ideological opposite of Asian autocracy, as Aeschylus had done in *The Persians*, or even to give it quite the same moral authority he gives to Sparta. Democratic Athens, after all, had briefly sought an alliance with the Persians when it felt its autonomy threatened by Sparta (5.73), just as Persia had installed democracies in its subject Greek cities in order to gain support among the lower classes (6.43). Both states, that is, pursue a foreign policy based more on self-interest than political principle, and the Spartans are forced to take seriously the possibility that they might make common cause. And although Herodotus largely absolves the Athenians of the stain of the Persian entente, claiming that the deal had been struck by envoys acting on their own authority and was quickly repudiated back home, one would be hard put to imagine the Spartans ever becoming involved in such dishonorable dealings.

Herodotus's questions about the moral stature of Athenian-style democracy are mirrored in his deeply ambivalent characterization of the one Athenian prominent in the *Histories*, Themistocles. This most slippery and inscrutable of Greek leaders enters the scene midway through book 7, during the debate at Athens over how to interpret the oracle of the "wooden walls," and is introduced by Herodotus in a curious way: "There was among the Athenians a certain man who had recently arrived among the foremost citizens, whose name was Themistocles, said to be son of Neocles" (7.143). Much debate has arisen over the phrase "recently arrived among the foremost citizens" because Themistocles had in fact served in a leading office at Athens thirteen years before this. Does Herodotus mean to discredit him as an upstart or an untutored youth? Similarly, does the wording "said to be son of Neocles" imply that Themistocles sprang from an obscure lineage or, worse yet, did not know for certain who his father was? Or is the entire sentence, as some believe, more fanfare than snub— a tribute to the as-yet unproven leader who stepped into the breach and solved the oracle's riddle? Whatever tone one hears here, Themistocles is clearly being cast as the representative of a new political order, in contrast to the tradition-bound monarchy of the Spartans. Compare, for example, the way Herodotus introduces the Spartan king Leonidas a short while later: "Leading the whole army was the Spartan Leonidas, son of Anaxandrides, son of Leon, son of Eurycratides . . . " and so on for twenty generations, leading back ultimately to the god Heracles (7.204).

Themistocles steps to the fore in book 8 of the *Histories*, where he reveals, on the one hand, the cleverness and daring of a tactical genius, but on the other a shyster's capacity for advancing himself and deceiving others. Here is the modern politician par excellence: he takes credit for ideas that are not his (8.58, 8.109–10), skims off bribe money to line his pockets (8.5), and mouths pious sentiments in an effort to disguise his self-promotion (8.109)—all episodes to which Herodotus, perhaps heeding the slanders of the anti-Themistocles faction at Athens, gives an unusually negative spin. At the same time, Herodotus leaves no doubt that Themistocles' insistence on the Athenian naval buildup before Xerxes' invasion and his manipulation of the allied strategy at the battle of Salamis had been instrumental in winning the war. The duplicitousness and cunning of this complex figure are part and parcel of his effectiveness as a commander. Indeed, our last view of Themistocles in the *Histories* reveals the two-sidedness of his character: at Sparta, the Greek world's bastion of military honor, he is given a hero's welcome and is escorted to the borders by a band of three hundred picked men—"the only man we know of whom the Spartan citizens thus escorted" (8.124). But even in this triumphal moment, Herodotus allows a taint of self-interest to discolor his portrait, noting that Themistocles first made his journey to Sparta out of a "desire to be honored."

It has often been said, with justification, that Herodotus embodies in Themistocles the dynamic, aggressive, self-serving spirit of democratic Athens itself. He is the only Athenian characterized in depth by Herodotus, though this does not, in and of itself, authorize us to treat him as a representative of Athens or its government. But the qualities for which the Spartans choose to honor him, cleverness (*sophiē*) and suppleness (*dexiotēs*), would have been recognizable to the audience of the *Histories* as hallmarks of the Athenian nature. The same is true of the less honorable greed he displays in extorting money from Andros and other island states that had, of necessity, sided with the Persians before Salamis (8.111–12). Herodotus here comments that Themistocles "never ceased pursuing profit," using a verb, *pleonekteō*, that later becomes standard vocabulary in discussions of Athenian imperialism after the Persian Wars. It is perhaps also significant that the action in which Themistocles here engages, besieging the islanders with his fleet to enforce his demands for cash, anticipates Athens's use of naval superiority to demand tribute from its subjects, starting in the 460s.

Ultimately, though, the *Histories* is more interested in the moral and ethical crises of early-fifth-century Athens than in its role as pioneer of democracy or of Greek imperialism. Because of its geographical position outside the Peloponnese, Sparta's favored line of defense, and because of its past entanglements with the Persian empire, Athens faced decisions more complex and consequential than other Greek states did. Those to the north easily submitted before the Persian threat, while those to the south, through either conviction or compulsion, resisted; only Athens in the intermediate zone stood on the razor's edge, and on Athens's choice the course of the war largely depended. On two occasions, at the end of book 8 and the beginning of 9, Herodotus dramatizes confrontations between Athens and Sparta over this choice: in both, Athens sticks by her Greek partner even after being offered a tempting separate peace with Xerxes. Whether Athens would have stayed faithful to the Greek cause forever is doubtful; Herodotus suggests that its resolve had already begun to wane in the spring of 479, when the Spartans grudgingly agreed to fight outside the Peloponnese. Nevertheless, Athens held out for as long as was needed, and for this fortitude Herodotus bestows upon it a crown of glory:

> If someone were to call the Athenians the saviors of Greece, he would not fall short of the truth. . . . They were the ones

who chose that Hellas should remain free, and who roused the rest of the Greek world, whatever part had not yet gone over to the Persians, and who, along with the gods, pushed the Great King out. (7.139)

Athenian resolve, Herodotus justly claims, had won the war; but it was only Athenian, not Spartan, resolve that had been in question to begin with.

The *Histories*, then, unlike some other Greek treatments of the Persian Wars, offers neither easy antitheses between Asian servitude and European freedom, nor any simple guidelines for understanding political issues. Just as he refuses to stereotype the individual Asian monarchs, so Herodotus declines to depict monarchy itself, even the absolutist variety found among the Persians, as a moral evil pure and simple; neither does he exalt democracy as an unequivocal good. As a pragmatist he was more interested in how both systems functioned either to the benefit or detriment of the people governed by them and in how well they performed when they came into conflict. The invasion of Xerxes, in his eyes, had simultaneously revealed the worst flaws of Asian autocracy and the best that could be achieved by Greek pluralism when Athens and Sparta combined their complementary strengths. Even so, it was the unity of Asia under one king that had made it so strong to begin with, while the division and contentiousness of Greece had nearly ruined it forever.

XIII THE GREAT WAR
AND THE
GREAT AGE

HERODOTUS'S *HISTORIES* IS, BEYOND ALL ELSE, A WAR STORY. It takes warfare as its subject for the simple reason that this was the central and most compelling activity of the world in which its author lived. Most adult males in Herodotus's society, no matter what city-state they belonged to, would have fought in a war at least once, if not several times, during their lives. The poem this society prized most highly, Homer's *Iliad*, was also a war story, dominated by graphic and often gory descriptions of hand-to-hand combat; the vase paintings and sculptural reliefs it produced depict scenes from warfare perhaps more often than any other subject; even some of the events held at its hugely popular athletic festivals were based on military exercises. Herodotus, then, was merely representative of, or responsive to, the tastes of his age in producing a literary work based on a series of wars; it never occurred to him in writing the *Histories,* any more than it did to other Greeks of his day, to question whether war in itself was morally right or wrong or whether steps should be taken to eliminate it. War is worse than peace because it disrupts the normal order of society, as Herodotus allows Croesus to assert in book 1 (chapter 87) and as he himself says, indirectly, in book 8 (chapter 3); but war is a fact of life, as inescapable as it is endlessly fascinating.

Part of its fascination, then as now, lies in war's capacity to reveal human nature in its most extreme dimensions, whether moral or immoral, heroic or savage. The kind of war story an author tells depends greatly on which of these extremes he chooses to explore. The modern-day war film, for example, tends to plumb the depths of the human soul, to focus on the ways men become dehumanized, even bestialized, in combat situations; this type of drama well befits an age in which war often seems innately repugnant, and the ideal of pacifism, a word unknown to our language until this century, is widely shared. In films dating back a generation or two, however, combat tends to bring out the better angels of human nature and can even be glorified as the proving ground of patriotism and courage. Herodotus in the *Histories* stands somewhere between these stylistic extremes, though in general he is closer in spirit to the latter: he focuses on the valor or greatness of spirit displayed in the Persian Wars by both Greeks and barbarians rather than on moments of weakness or emotional collapse. He never shows us, as Thucydides, for instance, regularly does, the confusion and terror of troops as they enter a battle or the despair of those facing defeat. The bravery of the three hundred Spartans under Leonidas, who had stared unafraid into the face of death, clearly holds greater interest for Herodotus than the panic that led the Phocians, at the same battle, to abandon their post when surprised by the enemy (7.218).

And Herodotus does not depict the physical toll of warfare with anything like the grim realism of Thucydides or, for that matter, Homer. Whenever warriors are wounded in the *Iliad*, Homer shows us in lurid detail the mangling of their skin, tissue, and bone; the fragility of flesh is constantly displayed before us, for it is in this, the sacrifice of corporal beauty and strength, that tragic heroism lies. Thucydides, similarly, keeps us in mind throughout his history of the Peloponnesian War of the hunger, thirst, and disease that afflict those involved in the fighting; in particular, his depiction of a plague that ravaged Athens during that war puts before our eyes an almost unbearable picture of physical suffering. Herodotus prefers to keep things clean. When his Greeks and Persians fight, he keeps a respectful distance from the cut-and-thrust action of the front lines. A rare detail drawn from the bloody realities of these battles—the hands of Cynegirus lopped off with an axe as he held onto a Persian ship at Marathon (7.114)—only reminds us how much has elsewhere gone unsaid. This is a sanitized portrait of warfare, in which we are made aware neither of the physical privation endured by armies in the field, nor of the mutilation of their bodies in combat. Again one could compare Herodotus's treatment with that of old-style war movies of the 1940s and 1950s: when a soldier was shot in those films, the audience rare_y saw any blood or heard a cry of anguish.

If Herodotus does not share Homer's interest in the flesh-and-bone side of warfare, he does share with his great forerunner a love of its pageantry and pomp. He takes obvious delight in the spectacle of Xerxes' great army marching out of Sardis (7.40–41) and in the solemn roll call of its many contingents, each with its distinctive armor and weaponry, each led by its own commanders (7.61–99). This roll call has been compared to Homer's catalogue of ships in book 2 of the *Iliad*, and the comparison is apt: both passages have an incantatory rhythm that, like the beat of a military drum, helps build suspense before the actual clash of arms; and both convey, in a tone of reverent wonder, the sheer enormity of the forces taking the field. After all, Xerxes brought to Greece an army and fleet larger than any seen there before (even after the wild numerical exaggeration of the *Histories* has been factored in), and Herodotus cannot help but pause and admire them from time to time, much as Xerxes himself did on the banks of the Hellespont. Just before the battle of Thermopylae, Herodotus conducts yet another inventory, counting the forces off numerically this time instead of ethnologically (7.184–87); this passage, too, heightens the awe and exaltation inspired by massive displays of power. A similar heightening is achieved when, in the course of this census, Xerxes suddenly and anomalously gains a lofty patronymic, "son of Darius," and when, in the next chapter, he is lionized: "Among those many tens of thousands of men, none was worthier, either in beauty or stature, to hold that power than Xerxes himself" (7.187).

The heroic aspect of warfare is further enhanced in the *Histories* by recurring hints that the gods watch over or actually participate in the battles waged by men. Here, too, Herodotus is working with conventions familiar from Homer's *Iliad* and still visible, though of course in different forms, in recent war myths and dramas. He recounts how a godlike being was seen among the Greek ranks at Marathon (6.117), and how a spectral woman appeared before the Greek fleet at Salamis, urging them on to the attack (8.84). He also describes a supernatural dust cloud that foretold the Greek victory at Salamis (8.65) and a Persian soldier's foreboding of defeat before the battle of Plataea (9.16); for both portents, moreover, he cites named witnesses, as if eager to assure his audience of their credibility. These apparitions are meant not so much to show that the Greeks had God on their side—the divine figure at Marathon, after all, fought for the enemy—as to add to the sense of destiny surrounding the entire course of the war. There was a divinity shaping the ends of both Greeks and Persians, Herodotus suggests in passages like these, and the result of much rough-hewing by both was a result that neither could have expected. This is a less partisan treatment, in other words, than that of a famous fifth-century Athenian painting of Marathon, reportedly showing the gods and heroes, including Athena herself, helping to push the Persians into the sea. Greeks and Persians alike, in Herodotus's account, are seen as participants in a scheme that transcends their own designs and lends meaning and importance to their actions.

As a war story, then, Herodotus's *Histories* is tinged with nostalgia and looks back on the Greco-Persian conflict in something of the same spirit—and from much the same distance— as we today look back on World War II. The invasion of Xerxes was "the big one," the war on which everything rested and in which everyone was involved. While it was being decided the fate of mainland Greece, indeed, of all Europe, hung in the balance. Its battles, after Thermopylae at least, were all-out engagements in which both sides chose to put everything at stake and both sides fought until a clear resolution was achieved. There was no regrouping of the Persian navy after Salamis or of the army after Plataea, only rout and headlong flight. Thereafter, the balance of power between Greece and Persia shifted permanently. Future battles would be fought on Asian, not European, soil, with the Greeks now taking the offensive.

This spirit of decisiveness and all-out confrontation had made the Persian Wars a great human achievement, in the eyes of Herodotus and his generation. True, Thucydides, writing in the next generation, claimed even greater significance for the Peloponnesian War, the subject of his history, because it lasted longer (twenty-seven years, with a break in the middle) and caused more destruction to the Hellenic world; the Persian War, according to Thucydides' dismissive account, "had a quick resolution, with two sea battles [Artemision and Salamis] and two land battles [Thermopylae and Plataea]." Yet this, Herodotus might have replied, is precisely the point; there *was* a quick resolution, *and* it rested on only a few big battles. The Persian War had been a war of engagement, whereas the Peloponnesian War, from what Herodotus had seen of it by the time he published the *Histories*, was not. Athens and Sparta had entered into conflict cautiously, by slow degrees of escalation; the exact point at which war had begun was unclear to both sides; and, most remarkable of all, for a long time no battles took place between the principals, only raids, skirmishes, and fights by proxy among subject states. Thus, if Herodotus had been given the chance to answer Thucydides, he might have scoffed at the thought that this new form of war, hardly recognizable as war at all, eclipsed the Persian invasions in magnitude or importance. The modern character of the Peloponnesian War, the very factors that made it so fascinating to the strategic mind of Thucydides, must have only increased the nostalgia Herodotus felt for the more straightforward, more committed warfare of the past.

Of course, the head-on approach was not always the most intelligent, as the Persians learned to their woe. On three occasions Herodotus shows them declining to use flanking strategies or delaying tactics that would almost surely have succeeded in favor of full frontal attacks that failed. In book 7, Demaratus, the exiled king of Sparta, proposes to Xerxes a plan of action very much like later Athenian tactics in the Peloponnesian War: send an arm of the Persian fleet around to the Spartan rear and occupy the island of Cythera (7.235). Later, Artemisia, queen of the Asian Greek city of Halicarnassus, gives similar advice before Salamis, urging Xerxes to avoid an all-out battle and to sail for the Peloponnese. Finally, Mardonius himself, prior to the battle of Plataea, is urged by both his second-in-command, Artabazus, and his Theban allies to withdraw from the field and use bribes and diplomacy to obtain his objectives. But, as Herodotus comments,

> Mardonius's judgment was more forceful, and more obstinate, and absolutely unwilling to give way; he thought that his army was much stronger than that of the Greeks

and preferred to attack immediately rather than permit
more of the enemy to gather than had already gathered.
. . . Better to follow the Persian way, and attack. (9.41)

"The Persian way" ultimately led to disaster, but the disaster
was glorious, just as Mardonius is a glorious though misguided
warrior. Herodotus may not have known much about battles—
his descriptions are so vague as to suggest that he had never
seen one himself—but he loved a good charge on land or on
sea, and in the Persian War every major engagement had seen
such a charge.

Other reasons, too, might have led the Greeks of Herodotus's day to feel a certain nostalgia for the conflict with Persia.
This was the first and, as it turned out, the only occasion on
which the Greeks could rally around a single, unambiguous
cause. Bright lines had been drawn; though not all Greek cities
joined the defensive alliance, all had known that this was, as
Herodotus puts it, "the better way of thinking about Greece"
(7.145), and those that missed their opportunity later regretted
it. The enemy was distinctly recognizable, as was the cost of
submission: economic servitude and loss of autonomy. In the
face of such a clear and present danger, many of the Greeks ac-
knowledged their common Hellenism and agreed to work together to defend it—a natural enough development from our
point of view, but a monumental one for a culture that had
only recently devised even a common name for itself. The
theme of unity against a common foe is sounded by Herodotus
on several occasions, but it swells to a triumphant crescendo in
an Athenian speech at the end of book 8, rejecting the idea of
abandoning the Greek alliance: "There are many great reasons
that prevent us from doing this, even if we wanted to: first and
greatest, the statues and shrines of our gods that have been
burned and demolished, for which we must take the severest

possible revenge rather than come to terms with their destroyer; second, our common Greekness [to Hellenikon], based on shared blood, and shared language, and common temples and sacrifices of the gods, and concordant customs, which it would not be right for Athens to betray" (8.144). In the face of barbarian invasion, the racial subgroups into which the Greeks had traditionally divided themselves, Dorian and Ionian (cf. 1.56), had seemed to merge to form a new entity, here dubbed vaguely to Hellenikon, "that which is Greek," for lack of any other name. That union broke down soon afterward, however, and the conflict between Athens and Sparta once again fragmented the Greek world along Dorian–Ionian lines. Gone was the moral clarity of the Persian War days, the sense that there was a right side to be on.

One minor episode in the Histories, just prior to the battle of Plataea, illustrates these gone-but-not-forgotten aspects of the Persian Wars blown up to exaggerated, almost absurd proportions. During the long wait before either army would begin battle, the Greek leadership decides to shift their position so as to secure supplies of food and water. But this move takes them further away from enemy lines and so could be construed—as Mardonius later does construe it—as a retreat. Thus when King Pausanias gives the order to march, a crusty Spartan corps commander named Amompharetus, who had missed the council meeting at which the repositioning was discussed, refuses to obey: "He said he would not run from the foreigners, and that he refused to bring disgrace on Sparta" (9.52). As Pausanias and his coregent plead with him to go along with their plan, Amompharetus picks up a boulder and hurls it at their feet, declaring that he thus casts his "pebble"—Greek citizens often voted by using pebbles as ballots—against retreating even an inch. In the end, Pausanias decides to proceed with the maneuver and leave the obstinate Amompharetus behind. The whole scene is staged by Herodotus in affectionate detail, such that Amompharetus is even given a peculiarly Spartan turn of speech when he calls the barbarians "foreigners." His defiance may have been comically mistimed, but one still feels that Herodotus stands on the side of this stalwart patriot, whose unwillingness to give ground and whose uncompromising hatred of the foreigners represent, in caricature, the best qualities of the Persian War generation. And in his tossing of the boulder-sized pebble, one hears an echo of Homer's account of Trojan War heroes, men capable of hurling stones so large that even nine latter-day warriors could not lift them.

Not only the Greek world but Asia, too, had entered a new era after Xerxes' invasion, an era that Herodotus does not discuss but that other observers describe as one of decadence and decline. The martial virtues that had made the Persians rulers of Asia seemed to give way to softness, idleness, and love of luxury; Persian nobles no longer took the field to expand the empire but dallied at home with their wines, fine clothes, and well-stocked harems. Thus the people who first appear in the *Histories* as a rugged race bred in a rugged land (1.71) soon grew so far removed from their stony origins that, according to one fourth-century writer, they required soft cushions everywhere, even strewn beneath their down-covered beds. It is perhaps with this decline in mind that Herodotus ends the *Histories* by relating a short anecdote from the time of Cyrus: offered the chance to move the Persians to level, fertile soil, Cyrus predicts that by doing so he would end their imperial rule, for "soft men tend to arise from soft countries; the same land cannot produce both wondrous fruits and men courageous in war" (9.122). Many who had observed the changes in Persian society since the defeat of Xerxes or indeed since the building of Darius's palaces on the level plains of Susa and Persepolis would have regarded Cyrus's dictum as a prophecy.

The Greeks who looked back at the early fifth century, then, saw an age of events larger than life, men made of steel, heroism of superhuman dimensions; and those who had survived the cataclysm of those days soon elevated its significance to the level of myth. Only eight years after Xerxes' defeat at Salamis, Aeschylus, a veteran of the battle, staged *The Persians,* one of only two or three Greek tragedies to take history rather than myth as its subject. Painters and lyric poets, who like the tragedians tended to focus on mythic themes, began to draw on the Persian Wars for their odes and murals. In the cities that had lost men in battle, shrines were erected and rites were performed to memorialize the dead, conferring on them the same semidivine status that attached to the heroes of legend. The three hundred Spartans killed at Thermopylae became the focus of an important cult center in Sparta, and an extant poem composed by the lyric bard Simonides is thought by some to have adorned their cenotaph. It begins,

> For those who died at Thermopylae
> Fortune was glorious, noble their doom;
> Their tomb is an altar, our grief their memorial, our pity
>   their praise.

Finally in the mid-420s, in the city of Athens, the Persian Wars received the greatest mythification of all: on the acropolis, on the south wall of the temple to Athena Nike (or Athena goddess of Victory), a sculptural frieze was erected depicting Greeks and Persians in combat, presumably at the battle of Marathon or Plataea. The friezes of Greek temples had depicted many battles before now: mythic struggles pitting the gods against giants, human heroes against centaurs, and Greek armies against the Asiatic enemies of the distant past, the Trojans or Amazons. The defeat of Xerxes now took its place among those ancient and sacred struggles, represented by some of the most graceful marbles that classical Athens ever produced. Those marbles, though badly damaged by time, can still be admired today in the British Museum, and in the temple of Athena Nike on the acropolis replicas have replaced the originals. Here, Greek hoplites, depicted naked (in accord with convention) except for helmets and billowing capes, grapple with leather-clad, quiver-bearing Persians; around the corner, on the eastern facade of the temple, an assembly of gods looks on in serene approval.

Also in Athens in the mid-420s, the comic poet Aristophanes staged his play *The Clouds*, a bitter satire on the changing moral values and progressive educational program of his day. In the play's climactic scene, two allegorical figures representing the old and new social orders vie for the loyalty of a youth named Pheidippides. The spokesman for the old order describes for this young man what he will gain if he schools himself in the old-fashioned way: respect for his elders, grace and decorum in music and drama, physical vigor, sexual modesty. The new-order spokesman, however, objects that such things are as outdated as the most obsolete of ancient festivals. "Nevertheless," his opponent declares, "these are the things with which our educational system brought up the men who fought Marathon." Aristophanes here rallies all the social virtues that he felt Athens was in danger of losing and sets them under the banner of the *Marathōnomachai*, the "Marathon-fighters," on whose shoulders the fate of the city had once rested. But then, as the scene reaches its dark conclusion, he sends that banner down to defeat. The schoolmaster of the old order turns out to be a fraud and a sexual libertine, and Pheidippides goes over to his modernist rival. The virtuous past represented by Marathon, now painted in more luminous colors than ever, cannot, from this play's perspective, be restored.

We cannot know for certain whether Herodotus lived to see either Aristophanes' staging of *The Clouds* or the sculpting of the Athena Nike temple frieze; neither can we know whether his *Histories*, probably already in circulation by the time these works were begun, helped to inspire their creators. But inevitably all three must be seen as products of a single moment, about half a century after the close of the Persian Wars—the moment, not coincidentally, when the last veterans of those wars were passing from the scene. The goal Herodotus claimed for himself in the opening sentence of the *Histories*, to prevent the deeds of humankind from losing their color with the passage of time, is the goal of a man who saw the world of the past slipping away, along with the generation who had shaped it. He himself had grown up in a different world but he had learned to revere that of his father. Without doubt he knew it could not be brought back, but he also ensured it would not be forgotten.

BIBLIOGRAPHICAL NOTE AND ACKNOWLEDGMENTS

THE READER WHO APPROACHES HERODOTUS TODAY IN ENGLISH TRANS-lation has several alternatives to choose from, most of them good ones. The Penguin edition, translated by Aubrey de Selincourt, can still be recommended more than forty years after its initial publication; the prose is too elevated and proper for Herodotus's style, but it reads well and conveys the author's meaning clearly and straightforwardly. Better still, a new edition has been issued (1996) with expert notes and revisions by John Marincola. In recent years, however, this old standard has been challenged by the new version of David Grene (Chicago, 1987), which uses a less lucid but livelier prose style and attempts to recreate in English the feel of Herodotus's peculiar Greek. The distinction between the two approaches is explained by Grene in his introduction: "The English in which [Herodotus] now speaks to us must have a flavor . . . that is as traditional and literary and a little archaic as Homer sounded for the fifth-century Greek," he asserts, whereas "the Penguin Herodotus sounds exactly as though new-minted by a twentieth-century journalist." Over the years I have found that some readers prefer the former approach, some the latter, depending on the degree to which they are willing to tolerate occasional obscurity for the sake of linguistic fidelity. Another, even more recent translation to be considered is that of Walter Blanco, in the Norton Critical Editions series (New York, 1992), which comes accompanied by a set of valuable critical essays edited by the translator and by Jennifer Tolbert Roberts. Unfortunately, this version offers only excerpts from the *Histories*, amounting to something less than half the original text; but the style is free and colloquial, and the accompanying glossary will be of great help to readers unfamiliar with Greek civilization.

As a way of comparing these three widely available translations, I have collected here their three differently flavored versions of a single sentence in Herodotus, from the end of Solon's speech to Croesus (1.33):

> De Selincourt: "Look to the end, no matter what it is you are considering. Often enough God gives man a glimpse of happiness, and then utterly ruins him."

> Grene: "But one must look always at the end of everything—how it will come out finally. For to many the god has shown a glimpse of blessedness only to extirpate them in the end."

> Blanco: "You have to see how everything turns out, for god gives a glimpse of happiness to many people, and then tears them up by the very roots."

I have not included in this group of recommended texts the George Rawlinson translation of 1858, still reprinted in the Everyman's Classical Library and Modern Library series; a classic in its day, its archaic diction (including "thee" and "thou" in passages of quoted speech), while not alien to the spirit of Herodotus's Greek, will nonetheless leave many readers cold.

Those wishing to pursue the historical questions raised by Herodotus's text or seeking a better understanding of the political and military maneuvers it records can consult the companion to the Penguin edition by Stephen Usher, *Herodotus: The Persian Wars* (Bristol, England, 1988); but this covers only the second half of the work and skips over some portions at that. The plain fact is that the *Histories* in its entirety covers so much turf, including both Greek and Near Eastern history, that few modern commentators feel competent enough to tackle it. As a result, no comprehensive work has appeared since W. W. How and H. J. Wells, *A Commentary on Herodotus* (2 volumes, Oxford, 1912), still an invaluable resource for those who know some Greek; its introduction, appendices, and maps are accessible to those without Greek and offer concise but detailed treatments of separate topics relevant to the *Histories*. Otherwise, the colorful narrative history by A. R. Burn, *Persia and the Greeks* (London, 1962), is organized so as to follow the narrative of the *Histories*, as is Peter Green's *The Greco-Persian Wars* (Berkeley, 1996, a revision of his earlier *Xerxes at Salamis*).

Good general studies of Herodotus include *Herodotus* by John Gould (in the Historians on Historians series, New York, 1989), *Herod-*

otus, Father of History, by J. L. Myres (Oxford, 1953), and *Herodotus the Historian* by K. H. Waters (Norman, Okla., 1985); all three focus rather more prominently on Herodotus's historiographical side than I have done here, but all are valuable, and Waters's book in particular is also highly entertaining. Another excellent resource for those interested not only in Herodotus the author, but early-fifth-century Greek culture in general, is Aubrey de Selincourt's *The World of Herodotus* (London, 1962), an eloquent and affectionate, indeed sometimes overromanticized, survey of many topics connected to the *Histories*. The structure and themes of the *Histories* are dealt with in a comprehensive fashion by Henry Immerwahr's *Form and Thought in Herodotus* (Cleveland, 1966; reprinted 1986), a dense but rewarding study, and by Donald Lateiner's *The Historical Method of Herodotus* (Toronto, 1989). In addition, the classical journal *Arethusa* published a special volume entitled "Herodotus and the Invention of History" in 1987, a collection of papers by diverse authors; though some of its essays are on specialized topics and require a knowledge of Greek, others (in particular those of Carolyn Dewald and Kurt Raaflaub) will intrigue nonclassicists, and it opens with a very useful summary of trends in recent Herodotean scholarship.

The vast range of specialized questions and subtopics raised by the *Histories* can best be pursued by starting with the bibliography to Waters's book, which is sensibly divided into twelve separate sections according to theme. However, I would call attention here to three works that have generated particular interest and, in one case, controversy. Stewart Flory's *The Archaic Smile of Herodotus* (Detroit, 1987), which focuses on the anecdotes and interpolated tales of the *Histories*, and François Hartog's *The Mirror of Herodotus* (trans. Janet Lloyd, Berkeley, 1988), dealing with the Scythian ethnography in book 4, have shown what complex and meaningful patterns can emerge when one looks closely at particular sections of Herodotus's text. In a very different arena, Detlev Fehling's *Herodotus and his 'Sources'* (trans. J. G. Howie, Leeds, 1989), originally published in German in 1971, argues that some of the material that Herodotus claims to have learned from informants, especially people in foreign countries, was actually made up by him; according to this view, Herodotus frequently abdicated the historian's commitment to truth and wrote like a novelist, concealing his inventions behind false attributions. Though some scholars have treated this as a heretical book (for example, W. K.

Pritchett in *The Liar School of Herodotus,* Amsterdam, 1993), none have decisively refuted it; the jury as yet remains out on these crucial interpretive questions.

Finally, for those who know a little Greek or are willing to learn some, there can be no better author than Herodotus to encourage and motivate the study of the language. His style is famous for its loveliness and charm, yet his syntax is not difficult; often he is the first author students are introduced to when they have reached a reading level, and after more practice they begin to feel the giddy sensation of following his narrative with some fluency. Moreover, there are many excellent resources to aid those seeking to attain such fluency, including J. E. Powell's *A Lexicon to Herodotus* (2d edition, Hildesheim, 1977) and several fine commentaries on individual books. Only Homer, perhaps, can offer better assurance to the beginner that the labors of learning an ancient tongue will pay off both richly and soon.

I would like to acknowledge here the authors and teachers whose words and ideas I have referred to in the preceding chapters. John Herington's essay "The Poem of Herodotus," in the new series of *Arion* (vol. 1, 1992, p. 8), is my source for the metaphor of the *Histories* as centaur (chapter I), and for much inspiration as well. Donald Kagan, in whose Greek history course I first read Herodotus, acquainted me with the long-cherished pun concerning Medes and Persians (chapter III). From Kurt Raaflaub's "Herodotus, Political Thought and the Meaning of History," another essay in the *Arethusa* volume quoted above, comes the quote in chapter IV about the subtext of Athenian empire in the *Histories,* though the thesis it represents is more fully articulated by Charles Fornara's *Herodotus: An Interpretive Essay* (Oxford, 1971). The comparison of the *Histories* to the *Guinness Book of World Records* in chapter VIII is taken from Kenneth Waters's book, cited above. An article by Stewart Flory, "Arion's Leap: Brave Gestures in Herodotus" (*American Journal of Philology* 99, 1978) is the source of the last of the Arion interpretations referred to in chapter VIII. The quote from Aubrey de Selincourt concerning Herodotus's style (chapter VIII) comes from *The World of Herodotus,* p. 27 of the edition cited above. The parallel between Thales' role in archaic Greek legend and Merlin's in Arthurian romance (chapter IX) is taken from the How and Wells commentary cited above, vol. 1, p. 94. The assessment of Xerxes' character quoted in chapter XI can be found in J. A. S.

Evans, *Herodotus, Explorer of the Past* (Princeton, 1991), p. 67. The passage from Matthew Paris's *Chronica Maiora* quoted in chapter XII was taken from the unidentified translation published in *Contemporaries of Marco Polo* (New York, 1989), edited by Manuel Komroff.

My thanks go out to those who have helped in the preparation of this book, and above all to John Herington, who as a teacher first planted in me the desire to study Greek literature and who has now, two decades later, helped that plant bear fruit. Sadly, he did not live to see the publication of this volume or the completion of the Hermes series that he directed from its inception. That series well represents the qualities that made John a beloved teacher and colleague and a peerless editor: profound expertise combined, as it so seldom is, with breadth of vision, creativity, humanity. His guidance on *Herodotus,* a volume he initially planned to write himself, has been invaluable to me, and I can only hope that the finished version lives up to the standards he set for it. Responsibility for any errors in the book remains my own.

Other assistance came from John Marincola, Walter Blanco, and John Pruitt; and the authors of previous Hermes books served as both models and inspirations, whether they knew it or not. Finally, I wish to acknowledge the generous help and tireless patience of my wife, Tanya Marcuse, to whom the book is dedicated; it was she who introduced me to *The English Patient,* and the epigraph to chapter I taken from it is for her.

INDEX

Achilles, 24 f.
Adrastus, 68 f.
Aeschylus, 68, 72; *The Persians*, 75, 166, 168, 170, 174–6, 186, 200; *Oresteia*, 85
Aeneas, 170
Aesop, 15–17
Alcmaeon, xv, 166
Alcmaeonids, 124
Amasis, 61 f., 69 f., 163–5
Amazons, 170 f., 200
Amompharetus, 198 f.
Anaxagoras, 141, 146
Anaximander, 14
Anaximenes, 14
Androphagi, 106 f.
"Ants" in India, 78, 139
Apollo, 3. *See also* Delphi
Apries, 164
Arimaspians, 78
Aristeas, 138
Arion, 117–19, 123
Aristagoras, 149
Aristophanes, 144, 146, 201 f.
Aristotle, 9, 11, 15, 49
Artabanus, 62, 86, 113; dialogues with Xerxes, 146 f., 167–9
Artayctes, 86
Artaynte, 170
Artemisia, 50, 171 f., 196
Asia: expansionist tendencies, 37; as Persian dominion, 82; distinct from Europe, 81–7, 173–5; weaponry and tactics of, 152; monarchy prevalent in, 179–85
Athena, 143
Athena Nike, temple of, 200 f.

Athens, 37; influence on Herodotus, 52–5; imperialism of, 52 f.; religious controversies in, 141; relations with Persia, 150–52, 189 f.; relations with Sparta, 153–6, 197 f.; democratic system of, 185–90
Athenians, 96
Atossa, 23, 174 f.
Atys, 3, 160 f.
Aztecs, 108

Babylon, 51, 80 f.
Babylonians, 34 f., 38, 99
Bacchylides, 2, 4
Bakis, 144 f.
Barbaros ("non-Greek"), 85 f., 95 f., 97
Biology in *Histories*, 66–8, 123 f.
Bosporus, 37, 46, 81–3. *See also* Hellespont

Cambyses, 3, 41–4, 72 f., 98, 109 f., 182, 184; and Croesus, 162; madness of, 163
Candaules, 120, 128
Cartography, xiv, 89–93
Causality 21–4
Cicero, 9
Cleomenes, 180, 182, 186
Cnidos, 79
Columbus, Christopher, 18, 109
Croesus, 20, 105, 166, 191; historical figure treated as myth, 1–4; historical career, 35, 37, 39; as paradigm of downfall, 60, 63–5; as tragic hero, 68 f.; portrayed by Herodotus, 159–62, 169

HERODOTUS

James Romm

Herodotus, widely known as the father of history, was also
described by Aristotle as a *mythologos,* or "tale-teller." In this
stylish and insightful book, intended for both general readers and
students, James Romm argues that the author of the *Histories*
was both a historian—in the original sense of "one who inquires"—
and a master storyteller.

Although most ancient historians wrote only about events they
had themselves lived through, Herodotus explored an era
well before his own time—from the rise of the Persian Empire to
the Persian invasions of Greece in 490 and 480 B.C., the heroic fight
of the Greeks against the invaders, and the final Greek victory.
Working without the aid of written sources, Herodotus traveled
widely and wove into his chronology descriptions of people and
countries he visited and anecdotes that shed light on their lives
and customs. Romm discusses the historical background of
Herodotus's life and work, his moralistic approach to history, his
insatiable fascination with people and places, his literary powers,
and the question of the historical "truth" behind the stories he
relates. He gives general readers a fresh appreciation of the *Histories*
as a work encompassing fiction and nonfiction, myth and history,
and poetry and prose. Herodotus becomes not simply a source
of historical data but a masterful and artistic author who created a
radically new literary genre.

James Romm is visiting associate professor of classics at Fordham
University and a Guggenheim Fellow.

HERMES BOOKS
John Herington, Founding Editor